Healing the Heart of a Nation

LAURA GAGNON

Copyright © 2016 Laura Gagnon

All rights reserved.

ISBN:1532740069
ISBN-13:978-1532740060

DEDICATION

This book is dedicated to all those who are searching for truth, healing and freedom, for yourselves and your families. I pray the Lord grant you revelation as you read through the pages of this book. May you discover the truth that sets you free.

This book or parts thereof may not be reproduced in any form, stored in a retrieval systems, or transmitted in any form by any means – electronic, mechanical, photocopy, recording or otherwise – without prior written permission of the publisher, except by United States of America Copyright law.

Scripture quotations marked NKJV are from the New King James Version, Copyright © 1982 by Thomas Nelson. Used by permission. All rights reserved.
Scripture quotations marked AMP are from the Amplified Bible, Copyright © 19541964, 1987 by the Lockman Foundation. Used by permission.
Scripture quotations marked CEV are from the Contemporary English Version, Copyright ©1995 by the American Bible Society. Used by permission.
Scripture quotations marked ESV are from the Holy Bible, English Standard Version, Copyright ©2001 by Crossway Bibles, a division of Good News Publishers. Used by permission.
Scripture quotations marked KJV are from the King James Version of the Bible. Used by permission.
Scripture quotations marked MSG are from The Message: The bible in Contemporary English, Copyright © 1993, 1994, 1995, 1996, 2000, 2001, 2002. Used by permission of NavPress Publishing Corp.
Scripture quotations marked NASB are from the New American Standard Bible, Copyright ©1960, 1962, 1963, 1968, 1971, 1972, 1973, 1975, 1977, 1995 by the Lockman Foundation. Used by permission.
Scripture quotations marked NIV are from the Holy Bible, New International Version, Copyright ©1973, 1978, 1984, 2011 by Biblica, Inc. Used by permission of Zondervan. All rights reserved worldwide, www.zondervan.com. The NIV and New International Version are trademarks registered in the United States Patent and Trademark Office by Biblica, Inc.
Scripture translations marked NLT are from the Holy Bible, New Living Translation, Copyright © 1996, 2004, 2007. Used by permission of Tyndale House Publishers, Inc, Wheaton IL 60189. All rights reserved.

CONTENTS

1	The Secret of Wisdom	Pg # 11
2	Unlikely Candidates	Pg # 21
3	Knowing Your History	Pg # 30
4	Restoring Foundations	Pg # 43
5	Demonic Foundations	Pg # 73
6	Identifying the Strongman	Pg # 96
7	Demonic Root Systems	Pg #140
8	Committing to Spiritual Growth	Pg #166
9	The Power of the Decree	Pg #170
10	A New Form	Pg #182
11	Prayers and Declarations	Pg #192

ACKNOWLEGEMENTS

I don't claim to be an expert on anything written within these pages. I can really only write from the things I've learned, been healed and delivered from, on my own personal journey, which covers quite a bit. I am simply a woman that loves God and responded to an unusual stirring to research, write and share my thoughts on the enormous task of healing the heart of our nation. Many experiences from my own journey are incorporated into the pages of this book. Why God chose me for this I am not entirely sure, but I'm not the first, nor will I be the last person to write on this subject. I pray that it will be a blessing to those that digest these truths and apply them to their lives. Writing this book was not a preconceived idea, but it became a labor of love for God and a call to a very special assignment.

While I realize that some of what I've written in these pages may be considered controversial, it has never been my intention to share what I've learned in order to offend. I know firsthand how discouraging it can be to suffer and struggle with demonic torment, physical infirmity, and bondage that seems to never end. My only hope in sharing what's in these pages is to help bring light and truth to others so that they can experience the same healing and freedom that I've been able to obtain – and I know there is so much more ahead, too!

I also realize, as I hope you do too, that we must each search our own hearts with honesty and recognize the need to deal with things that may become evident upon reading a book of this nature. It is not always easy or enjoyable to face the reality of things we have opened a door to, or perhaps an ancestor opened a door to, that is still affecting our lives today. This book is full of historical facts as well as spiritual truth, much of which has been made available through the research and writings of others. I would like to acknowledge my appreciation for the efforts others have gone through to also share the rich truths given to them by God, their personal experiences, and their obedience to fulfill their calling. I would like to extend my respect and gratitude towards Christian leaders such as John Eckhardt , Cindy Jacobs, Drs. Jerry and Carol Robeson, Chuck Pierce and others that have enriched the body of Christ with their teachings on spiritual warfare. For all those that have played an integral part in my own spiritual journey, I thank you and honor you.

INTRODUCTION

Generations of people from every nation, race and culture suffer needlessly from unbroken curses. Those effects have shaped the world that we live in today.

Many people would be grateful and appreciative of anyone that would come share with them how they can break free from things that cause poverty, hopelessness and a sense of defeat. We do not have to live with broken hearts and broken lives. Addictions can be broken. Relationships can be healed. Finances can be restored. Sickness can be healed. Even the areas of our lives that have been robbed by the spirit of death can be healed and restored, if we will take the time to learn of God's ways and apply them to our lives. He has a better plan, revealed through the pages of this book.

God's plan for each person, each city and nations is redemption, revival and restoration. Each chapter will take you through a different part of His plan, but also share some shocking historical and spiritual truths that reveal the enemy's tactics to hinder God's ultimate plan. Satan has taken people into captivity, and attempted to steal the destiny of our families. I hope you will agree, as I do, that Satan's day of reckoning is long past due and it's time to recover our losses. It's time to put our foot down on the enemy's head and let him know, "NO MORE PLUNDERING. I WANT WHAT'S MINE, NOW GIVE IT BACK!!"

Together we will explore historical facts that reveal the deception of the enemy that has literally *in*fected and *aff*ected multitudes of families in our nation. We will also examine God-given wisdom and strategies that will reverse the curse and allow people to recover the blessings of God that are theirs by right of inheritance.

CHAPTER ONE
THE SECRET OF WISDOM

" There was a small city with few men in it and a great king came to it, surrounded it and constructed large siege works against it. But in it was found a poor wise man and he delivered the city by his wisdom. Yet no one remembered that same poor man." Ecclesiastes 9:15

That verse of scripture has been a topic of prayer between the Lord and I over the course of several years. Something caught my attention when I read this verse. One little, seemingly inconsequential man had the wisdom to deliver his city. One man. Delivered a city.

I'm intrigued. I want to know more!

No one remembers his name. Yet somehow he discovered the secret to releasing such breakthrough and deliverance that it brought healing to an entire city.

What was his secret?

What was his prayer life like?

Why did God choose him?

What was the strategy God used to deliver that city?

The city had a problem. A powerful king had brought an unstoppable military operation against the city and it was surrounded by enemy troops. The chief magistrates, military personnel and the ruler of the city had exhausted themselves arguing over strategy. The so-called 'wise men' had all struck out and were out of answers. The citizens were faced with an ominous threat and an impossible situation. That is exactly the type of situation that attracts the attention of heaven! Now that the stage had been set; it was God's cue to step in!

God was waiting for that moment. I can just imagine Him kicking back, putting His feet up and munching on a bowl of popcorn as He watched the show. *The really big show.*

One by one, He watched the wisest of the wise attempt to figure out a way to save the city. The local intelligence committee (looking more like an episode of The Three Stooges) came up short. Meanwhile, the king that was known as *Mr. Too-Big-For-His-Britches* had made some malicious moves that made the townspeople panic. Food and supplies had been cut off for weeks, and people were getting testy. Riots ensued. Guards were having a tough time keeping peace among the captives. The vainglorious windbag of a king proudly boasted of his accomplishments, thinking the victory was in the bag. Big mistake! The king that felt oh-so-assured forgot there was One who was even more powerful than him. **He** had watchers everywhere who were constantly reporting in; nothing escaped Him. He saw everything, and to Him, the whole situation struck Him as ridiculously amusing.

"The Lord laughs at him, For He sees his day is coming." Psalm 37:13 NIV

With a burst of laughter THE KING hits pause on the universal remote and pushes a button on the intercom. *"Send in the little guy, please. The one over there on the bench!"* A chipper and overly enthusiastic angel runs out the door, practically tripping over his own feet to reach God's newest unsuspecting recipient of unexpected favor. The King of Kings was about to wipe the smug look off of the tyrant's face and give him a taste of his own medicine. The angel, wondering how the unsuspecting servant would feel when he found out that he had been chosen for a very important assignment, was bursting with good news!

There isn't really a story to accompany the verse in Ecclesiastes 9:15, but one thing I know is God used an unassuming man to bring wisdom to a problematic situation when no one else had the answers. The mighty adversary, who thought he had the perfect plan to lay siege against the city and destroy the lives of its citizens, was outsmarted by an insignificant person, probably not even on his radar. So insignificant in fact, that no one even remembered his name afterwards. We don't know the rest of the details as to how his plan was carried out, but that doesn't matter. Whatever that man said was the strategy needed at the moment, and it worked. What we do know is that God chose an unlikely person to lead others into action and they victoriously took their city back from the enemy. It is a good lesson for all of us that God's wisdom far supersedes human wisdom.

If the king, bent on destruction, represents Satan, then the poor man represents Christ. Humility in a well-chosen vessel will outwit the schemes of the enemy and our adversary any time.

"For I will give you words and wisdom that none of your adversaries will be able to resist or contradict." Luke 12:15 NIV

There's something different about godly wisdom that bears

witness in the human heart. The secret of the poor man was his smallness. Smallness speaks of humility. The unassuming person doesn't look like a threat to the proud, arrogant person who has forgotten God. Remember the story of David and Goliath? Goliath laughed when he saw little David running up to him with nothing more than a prayer and a slingshot, and he mocked him. The giant was actually offended that King Saul would send in someone so inconsequential. He expected someone that he considered better qualified to fight with him. Yet, it was God that led David to the battlefield that day. David's smallness allowed him to get close enough to the situation that he was able to take down the giant. David was so embarrassed by the lack of leadership in Saul's army and the arrogance of Goliath's threats, it stirred a reaction inside of him. He *had* to get involved, and later he discovered that he had somehow just earned hero status. A small and seemingly insignificant man walked onto the field, but a warrior left the battlefield holding the enemy's severed head. David wasn't looking for attention; He just couldn't stand the enemy standing there mocking His God. God saw David's heart and it pleased Him, so He gave him an opportunity to make a difference. God gives grace and assistance to the humble in order to outwit the proud. Humility shows that a person is teachable, and God can pour in His wisdom to those that are willing to humble themselves before Him.

God can do it again, and He wants to do it with you! As a matter of fact, God has been doing it again and again using a single person here, there and everywhere to bring healing and deliverance to anyone willing to receive. Healing a nation is not so different than healing a city. In each chapter you will find insights, strategies and keys to healing and delivering families, communities, and cities. If we can heal our cities, we can heal our nation. How do you deliver a city? By releasing healing and deliverance to families. How do you heal families? You start with the one.

One person in a family can become the catalyst to spur others on towards their own healing and deliverance. One little firebrand who has caught on fire for Jesus has the potential to set a fire in their family, neighborhood and city, sharing testimonies, experiences, hope and the love of God. This is how we bring transformation and cultural change.

"Blessed are the poor in spirit, for theirs is the kingdom of heaven." Matthew 5:3

The poor in spirit are those who humbly acknowledge their need to be led. They recognize their own personal weaknesses and don't think too highly of themselves. They don't revel in their popularity, achievements, gifts or abilities, but seek after their

Redeemer. The poor in spirit acknowledge their need for wisdom and guidance, and willingly submit to the leading of God's Spirit. The poor man represents a person who isn't full of their own ego and accomplishments, but is small in their own eyes. The poor wise man in Ecclesiastes 9:15 was a man that was humble and sincere in his desire to see his city turn over a new leaf. He could see the bondage, the oppression and the spiritual poverty of those around him that lived apart from God. I believe it really bothered him. It probably kept him up at night. Why else would he feel the burden of wanting to see his city delivered?

Every person has certain qualities about them that are useful for solving problems. Past experience, training and wisdom that is picked up along the way helps us develop a unique skill set that is uncommon and particular to each individual. We use all of it when reasoning out how to tackle problems. One thing that also becomes a factor are the things we've been through. The greatest advocates for freedom and justice are those that understand the pain and affliction that others are going through. God knows what our hot-buttons are, and what will stir up a reaction in us. God uses the things we can't ignore to pull reluctant bystanders into situations He wants to fix. God knows this about us because He created us. He knows what makes us tick, and what gets under our skin. He knows how to get our attention. What about you? What stirs your passion?

When God wants to use a particular person to solve a God-sized problem, He has to first get their attention. He will poke and prod at a person until they feel compelled to get involved. He wants us to feel the burden of those that He cares about. He wants us our hearts to be moved with compassion over the things that touch His heart.

I don't know what it took to get the attention of the man in Ecclesiastes 9:15, but I know what it took to get mine. A whole lot of anger, stress, frustration and restlessness, spiritual battles, physical battles, depression and discouragement, to name a few. I wrestled with myself, my family, the Lord, and the strongman over my city for a long time before I finally realized that I was in some sort of spiritual tug-of-war. What I didn't realize for a very long time is that what I was attributing to natural issues of life were also tied into spiritual warfare. The strongman didn't want me praying for my city, but God did. I didn't find much enjoyment where I lived, so I was constantly feeling dissatisfied and frustrated. Stuck. Maybe in some ways I was acting a bit like Jonah, pulling in the wrong direction.

I had to repent before God would share His wisdom. Repentance is an act of humility towards God. I had asked for wisdom to deliver a city, yet truth be told, I really didn't have much desire to stay where God had put me. In my opinion, there isn't a lot to get excited about in my city. Every time our family looked for something to do we had to drive somewhere else to go find it. Now, that may not be true for everyone, but that's been true for us. Lack of answers and not really understanding why God planted us in this particular place added to my growing frustration. I felt like I was constantly looking for an escape.

I wasted a lot of time hoping, praying or wondering if God would move us somewhere else. I finally realized that He put me where I was with an assignment in mind and I wasn't being obedient to it, which I think had a large part in the spiritual warfare I had experienced. The spirit realm is quite aware when people are either submitted to God or not, and they are keen to discern when they have been granted an open door! My heart had not been in it to the degree that it should have, and God wasn't going to share His wisdom with me until I got my priorities right. My heart had not been committed to what I had asked for in prayer. God wants us to be *all in*. He's not pleased with someone that is looking for an opportunity to cut and run the moment challenges present themselves. He's looking for those who are fully committed.

"The LORD's eyes keep on roaming throughout the earth, looking for those whose hearts completely belong to him, so that he may strongly support them." 2 Chronicles 16:9 ISV

The moment I repented and confessed my disobedience to the Lord, not only did I have a sense of peace about where I was planted, but He began leading me to truth. Every fresh revelation was like opening a new box of hidden treasure. Those treasures of wisdom and understanding are included in this book for you to find. The need for *a greater level of humility* towards God was the first **key** to obtaining secrets that could only be found in Him. If people will stop, digest what is being shared, and engage with God over it, I believe together we will begin to open the heavens in our cities.

There is a parable in Matthew 13:44 that represents the kingdom of God. It tells of a man who discovered treasure hidden in a field. He was so excited about it that he sold everything he had in order to buy the whole field. God wants us to give all we have in order to discover the treasure of revelation that He has hidden in His word. The kingdom of God *is* the Pearl of Great Price. It's the poor in spirit who inherit the kingdom of heaven. The poor wise man humbly discovered the secret of buried treasure. Where is the treasure buried? *In the kingdom.*

CHAPTER TWO
UNLIKELY CANDIDATES

"Not many of you were wise by human standards; not many were powerful; not many were of noble birth. But God chose the foolish things of the world to shame the wise; God chose the weak things of the world to shame the strong. He chose the lowly and despised things of the world, and the things that are not, to nullify the things that are,..." 1 Corinthians 1:27

When God surveys new applicants for a job assignment, He doesn't always chooses the person who most people think is the best candidate for the job. While they may have a stellar reputation, a long list of accomplishments, great references and a top-notch resume, He looks for other more 'colorful' qualifications. In the kingdom of God, it's often the person with a ruined reputation that gets God's attention. If yours isn't ruined yet, don't worry; He will get around to it sooner or later! Being misunderstood is pretty much par for the course. Rahab, Tamar,

Moses, Joseph, Sampson, Jonah and Saul are only a few Biblical examples of people God used in powerful ways, in spite of their reputations and personal weaknesses. Rahab was a harlot, Tamar got pregnant by her father-in-law, Moses was a murderer, Joseph was falsely accused and imprisoned, Sampson was a womanizer, Jonah was full of himself and ran from God - and let's not forget Saul of the New Testament. Saul was a religious zealot that persecuted Christians and had them killed (that was before the Holy Spirit got a hold of him). Saul would be the equivalent of an evil drug lord or an ISIS leader in our day. He was so spiritually blind that God actually had to make him blind for three days just to get his attention. Saul just never asked the right questions until the Lord pulled him up short and struck him blind. *That* got his attention! Saul's reputation spread far and wide and put fear in the hearts of other Christians, until they realized his conversion was authentic. My point is, God can use anyone to fulfill His purposes!

Lousy reputation? It's ok! Bad credit? No problem. Criminal history? Great! You just moved to the top of the list. No matter what black mark you've got against you or how many strikes against your record, YOU are just what He's looking for! Hard to believe, but true. I think it amuses Him to use the most unlikely person that others would never pick. God assigns value to people that others would write off. I like that about Him, don't you? God can indeed do what seems impossible to man and use the most unlikely people, whether we agree with His methods or not.

God intentionally chooses people whose names are synonymous with scandal, their reputations marred by unseemly tales of past failures. He likes shock value, because it makes it that much more difficult for others to believe when He does something absolutely grand in their lives. But, He also chooses ordinary people with ordinary lives to accomplish incredible things, sometimes through the power of simply loving others. How often it is that the giants we slay are the giants of despair, heartache, fear, and worry. Some days, the giants we slay aren't even out own. They're the giants in the lives of others.

One unsung hero is a high school physics teacher by the name of Jeffrey Wright. His students love him and never want to miss class because he makes class time so interesting and interactive. Mr. Wright slays giants on a daily basis.

Not only is he a great teacher, but he's a stand-out human being as well. He's approachable, compassionate and concerned about his students, and they know it. He radiates love, and in return, they have brought them their deepest secrets, their shame, their struggles and heartache. They pour out their stories because they know they can trust him. He's there for them.

What makes Mr. Wright's story even more compelling is the fact that he has openly shared his own disappointment about shattered dreams and anger towards God when his son, Adam, was born with a severely disabling disease known as Joubert Syndrome. Joubert Syndrome is defined by an underdeveloped brain stem and various developmental disabilities. The Wrights were told at his birth that Adam was born blind, and he cannot control his body's movements. He is completely intelligent, trapped in a body that is completely functional, at least on the internal aspects, but externally has failed him. His muscles do not receive the messages they need to tell them how to work together properly because his brain cannot communicate the correct signals. He can't even sit up on his own. His life is similar to that of a wheelchair bound paraplegic. Joubert Syndrome is so rare that only 417 people on the entire planet have this unfortunate condition.

Mr. Wright shared how his hope and dreams for his son's life were crushed, and how he struggled to understand why God would allow such tragedy to come to his innocent, infant son. His hopes of playing ball and enjoying ordinary father-son moments were stripped away before he ever had a chance to experience them. God didn't give him immediate answers to all his questions, but allowed Jeffrey to discover them on his own.

When Adam was a baby, they discovered that he wasn't blind

like they thought, and they began to teach him sign language. The day that Adam signed the message, "Daddy, I love you," changed Jeffrey's entire perspective. He was no longer mad at God. It was then that Mr. Wright figured out a very important life lesson. "That was when I figured out I didn't care *how* things work anymore; it was about *why* things work. Things work because of love," Wright said. "There's something a lot greater than energy, there's something a lot greater than entropy," Wright continued. "What's the greatest thing?" He asked his students. "Love." "It's why we exist."

"In that great big universe with all those stars," he says looking up, "you ask who cares?" "Well Somebody cares about you a whole lot," Wright said. "And as long as we love each other, that's where we go from here." [1]

"Mr. Wright has the key to the city," remarked student Denaz Taylor. Indeed he does. **Love is the key that wins hearts.**

* * *

Allow me to introduce you to another ordinary person doing

---

[1] Zack Conkle, Mr. Wright's Law of Love,
http://www.karmatube.org/videos.php?id=3723

extraordinary things. Her name is Wanda Steward, and she works on Obsidian Farm in Berkeley, California. In a short inspirational film titled, **Heal the Land, Heal the Spirit**, by Sid Woodward, Woodward writes, "Wanda Stewart shares her life as an urban farmer, educator and comrade to many in the movement to educate and inspire others to grow their own food and communities. She is committed especially to working with other African-Americans to re-frame the shattered history, trauma and greatness through the act of legacy gardening. Stewart explains how working outdoors is healing to her soul and spirit."

"When I come in from working outdoors," she says, "I am calm, relaxed and elated. I use my body in ways that are really resourceful. Just right there on that level, it's worth it," says Stewart. She describes what she does as ***essential.***

"I know there are so many lessons to be learned about how to live our lives," Wanda explains. "From how to grow your own seed – whether that's your own life, whether that's your child – but tending a garden is not different from tending a life."

"Stewart blends her skills in recruitment, community outreach, and program development with her passions for people and urban farming to model, inspire, and support whole life transformation - in individuals and in communities – through the act of gardening and the lens of African American culture and traditions." - S. Woodward

Wanda goes on to explain how thoughtful planning and 'heaps of faith' is the hope that something will come from her efforts to impart survival skills that teach people resilience. She talks about the progressive work in the garden, and the fact that how it appears today is not at all what it looked like 5 years ago, or even a year ago. In a mere moment she takes us back in time, recalling the crimes of past generations. "The garden," she explains, "was the scene of many crimes and trauma, where her people escaped, fleeing the plantations and fields where they had been slaves. We put a lot of horror behind us in doing that, but we also left wonderful things there. We forgot that we know how to grow things, that we could feed ourselves and we did eat well. I see these pictures of former slave women. One of them is 125 years old and she looks like she could keep up with me, for sure," Stewart says, laughing. "There's a lot we got out of there, a lot of greatness in that dirt, and we turned our back on it." [2]

Wanda explains that what she really feels it is all about is going back and tilling the soil again. She uses the metaphor of gardening

---

[2] Sid Woodward, Heal the Land, Heal the Spirit; www.karmatube.org/videos.php?id=5954

to illustrate issues of the heart and soul. Tilling the soil is a gardening term that cultivates the ground for new seed, but it goes down deeper than just the topsoil. Cultivating is a process that brings weeds up to the surface where they can be pulled out. It rids the soil of rocks, weeds, roots and other impediments that hinder the new seed from being able to grow.

I think what she's really trying to communicate through her gardening analogies is that even though people have left behind some things that caused them to endure trauma, pain or suffering, we have to revisit those areas of our lives to remember the good, too. There are some good memories and things we've learned along the way that have helped to enrich our lives. We can't afford to throw out the good along with the bad. We must allow ourselves to go back and remember the things that are profitable. It's ok to allow ourselves to forgive the past and move on. God wants us to do that. He wants us to trust Him to create a brand new future, and a brand new future has no room for bitterness. It's been said that we can change locations, but if we use the same bricks we used to build the old house, we'll end up building the same house all over again.

Bitterness is a thief that will steal away the good memories. When people cannot remember the good, then the negative memories become the dominant place holder in their memory bank. In no way do I suggest that the injustice of past events is not significant, but we can't allow those things to ruin us. Focusing on the negative things in life, blaming others and identifying with the role of a victim neither strengthens a person nor does it give a person peace. Those things actually have the ability to deplete us of spiritual, emotional and physical strength. Forgiveness, trusting God to help us build the life we desire, and remembering in whose image we are created are keys to a life of peace and joy.

Wanda Stewart has revisited her past and recovered her greatness, and now she inspires others by teaching them the lessons she's learned and applied to her own life. It's a reminder that we, too, can recover the abundance from our past, but real potency exists in our ability to demonstrate largeness of heart. If we want to move from feeling insignificant to significant, we must learn to love well. Greatness is given to us by God. It's our inheritance. It's our legacy, and with 'heaps of faith' we <u>will</u> recover all that belongs to us.

CHAPTER THREE
KNOWING YOUR HISTORY

Every city is known for something. Escondido, where I live, is one of the oldest original cities in San Diego county and used to be known for its rich agriculture. Grapes, avocados, oranges, lemons and walnuts were considered the most important agricultural products of the valley. Although it is still known for being an agricultural city, it's not what it once was. Like every other city, it has its problems. There is a curse on the land that has taken its toll in many ways: drought, poverty and financial hardship, homelessness and more.

Escondido is a Spanish word meaning 'Hidden.' One source says the name originally referred to Agua Escondida, or 'Hidden Water.' Another says it meant 'Hidden Treasure.' Settled by the

Luiseno Indians, they named it 'Mehel-on-pom-pavo.'[3] There is some uncertainty as to the translation, but some translations say it means 'rest from labor,' while other Native American tribes such as the Kumeyaay may have translated it to mean 'a place where it rains.' Neither of those things seem to be all that true today; that is the result of many accumulated generational curses.

The interesting thing is that both the Native American translations have a redemptive purpose, reflecting the truth found in the Bible. God would bring His people into the promised land of their inheritance, help them conquer the enemies of that land, and then they would enter the promise of His rest. They were told to 'take possession' of the land. Possessing the land meant they had to take ownership and responsibility for everything in that land. Since God owns everything, we become stewards of what actually belongs to Him. Every tribe was given a portion of the land as their inheritance, but they would have to fight for it. They would need to outwit, overcome and displace the enemies that took their inheritance and called it their own.

It's the same with us today. Wherever God has us positioned, we have a responsibility to possess the land and reclaim it for the

---

[3] Wikipedia, the Free Encyclopedia; Escondido, California, https://en.wikipedia.org/wiki/Escondido,_California

kingdom of God. But, we must identify with the people that are already there. We must learn to love our neighbors as ourselves, and treat them the way we would want others to treat us. Another part of identifying with the people of any given city is to also identify with the sin of that city, even if you weren't personally the one to commit those sins. This principle applies on a larger scale, too. We must also identify with the sins of our forefathers. The curse is on the people and the land *until* people take the time to repent and put those sins under the blood of Jesus. Only the blood of Jesus is powerful enough to purge the stain of sin, but where there is no blood covering, there is no forgiveness of sin. That is why it is so necessary to acknowledge the sin before God. He wants to cleanse us from the guilt and the curse that comes from disobedience, but we must agree to 1) ask for forgiveness and 2), turn away from it.

"If we claim that we're free of sin we're just fooling ourselves. A claim like that is errant nonsense. On the other hand, if we admit our sins - make a clean breast of them - He won't let us down; He'll be true to Himself. He'll forgive our sins and purge us of all wrongdoing. If we claim that we've never sinned, we out-and-out contradict God - make a liar out of Him. A claim like that only shows off our ignorance of God." 1 John 1:9,10. MSG

"...Stop sinning and do what is right. Break from your wicked past

and be merciful to the poor. Perhaps then you will continue to prosper." Daniel 4:27 NLT

"By lovingkindness and truth is iniquity atoned for, and by the Fear of the Lord one keeps away from evil." Prov. 16:6 NASB

"He who conceals his transgressions will not prosper, but he who confesses and forsakes them will find compassion." Prov. 28:13

That brings us to the next step, which is understanding the nature of generational curses, how they affect our culture, and how to break them through prayers of repentance.

You might be thinking, "Is it really necessary, or Biblical, to break generational curses?" "Isn't that Old Testament?"

Many people question whether confessing the sins of their ancestors is biblical, or necessary. Consider the fact that when the early church was first established (in the Book of Acts), there did not yet exist any other authoritative scripture outside of the Old Testament. That was their standard for sin, confession, conduct, and how to live. There are plenty of Old Testament scriptures that model identificational repentance, such as in Ezra, Nehemiah, Moses' and Daniel's examples of identifying with the people they were called to live among. They included themselves in the confession of sin, appealing to God for mercy and forgiveness on behalf of the nation. New Testament scriptures that speak of confession of sin are found in James 5:16 as well as 1 John 1:9. We learn that the principles of Old Testament law are not nullified in the New Testament, rather Jesus came as the fulfillment of the law. Jesus quoted the scriptures as a means of both rebuking the enemy and giving instruction.

"All Scripture is inspired by God and is useful to teach us what is true and to make us realize what is wrong in our lives. It corrects us when we are wrong and teaches us to do what is right." 2 Tim. 3:16 NLT

The principles of scripture must be seen through the lens of the cross, and what it came to afford us, but we still adhere to the principles found in God's word, according to scriptures in the Book of Romans. (see 3:31, 8:4 and 13:8).

God no longer punishes His children for the sins of their forefathers. However, the sin **weaknesses** and **sin patterns** of the parents will be visited upon the children. God doesn't do this; the enemy does. Familiar spirits entice, tempt and lure other family members into the sins that have already been committed, learned and practiced in an unsanctified lifestyle. This is how the curse passes down the bloodlines in families. God does not curse His children, but Satan *does*. And, though some things may not necessarily be transferred from our ancestors to us as punishment from God, we still have to deal with the things that existed prior to our salvation. Before we came into covenant with God, we were in a covenant relationship with Satan. We might not stop to think about it in those terms, but that is the truth. Before we came to Christ we were under the law of sin and death. Familiar spirits attach themselves to families and reproduce certain weaknesses towards sin, creating negative patterns of repeated loss, brokenness, generational poverty and other things. We don't have to be bound to the past. The way to break the curses is through repentance and confession of those sins, both of ourselves as well as identifying with the sins of our parents, grandparents and other ancestors.

Repentance pleases God because it restores people to right relationship with Him. It opens the heavens so that prayers are no longer blocked; communication between God and mankind is restored. Renouncing the sins of ourselves and our ancestors breaks generational curses, restores our ability to receive blessings from our heavenly father and dismantles ungodly authority structures. Repentance, which is the act of forsaking our sins and applying the blood of Jesus to them, enables us to de-throne evil rulers, weaken and dismantle ungodly authority structures, and deprives Satan of the worship he so desperately craves.

When people make sin habitual, it becomes a form of worshipping the enemy. I realize people don't wish to acknowledge that, but that is the spiritual reality. Sin is disobedience to God and it forms an agreement with spiritual forces of darkness. Demons want access to our lives and they look for any opportunity that grants them legal grounds to plunder our blessings. Over time, repeated sin becomes a place where Satan is worshipped. Maybe not openly, but through a person's actions and willingness to deny God's authority and Lordship in their lives. When people deny the ways of God, they accept another authority in their lives. They may think they are just living life on their terms, making their own decisions, but it is still a life lived apart from God. Living for self is a form of idolatry because a person's own ways become more important than accepting His loving guidance and wisdom for their lives.

The more spiritual darkness that exists in a place, the more that evil is empowered. A throne is a place where a god, sovereign or ruler is seated. A throne is where that entity is acknowledged and given authority, dominion and power. Sometimes people realize they are offering worship to an idol or a god; other times they may be unaware that their actions are a form of enthroning and empowering demons in their life.

All of these things are important and play a part in a city's culture, and how it manifests throughout our nation. A city takes on the personality of the people that came before them and those that are there now. Every time new people move into a city, they are building upon the foundations of those that came before them. They learn to adopt to that culture. The history of each city plays a significant role in shaping the culture that evolved and what it has become today. How and why the city was founded, historical events that took place during that time, the meaning of its name, the strongholds and problems within that city, as well as the redemptive purposes of God; all are symbolic and meaningful. Until people understand God's redemptive purpose, they won't be able to accurately speak into their city's true identity. If one isn't aware of their city's purpose they don't know how to call it forth. These are all principles that apply on a grand scale, impacting our nation as a whole.

Let me share some insights about my own city. Somewhere between the Native Americans who called Escondido 'Mehel-on-pom-pavo,'[4] the Mexican-American battle of San Pasqual in 1846, and the land grab in its formative years, lies Escondido's real identity. What was once known as *a place where it rains* and where people could *rest from their labor*, became known as the

---

[4] Escondido, California, Wikipedia Free Encyclopedia; https://en.wikipedia.org/wiki/Escondido,_California

Devil's Corner and the Devil's Lurking Place. Unfortunately, it also became a place known for human trafficking and many other things which allowed a false identity to emerge.

During 1843 a re-allotment of a parcel of land known as Rincon del Diablo was transferred over to Juan Bautista Alvarado. In the process, the name became known as the Corner of the Devil, and was somehow implied that whatever wasn't owned by the church and missions was owned by the devil.[5] So there you have it. There's a lot of truth in those words. Somebody's going to take ownership of the land. **If Christians won't fight for it, the devil will take it by default.**

Native Americans were the first to pioneer and settle the land. Many great atrocities have occurred against the Native American people throughout history. Every group of explorers and pioneers understandably sought to take over new lands and implement the customs of their native culture, but a great deal of the process involved in settling new lands in America was done with brutal disrespect of those that were already in the land and had made it their home.

---

[5] Dr. Rabee McDonald, *The Meaning of Escondido Lies Deep in San Diego History*, Oct. 9, 2014; https://www.ltsmiles.com/meaning-escondido-lies-deep-san-diego-history/

The Indian Removal Act of 1830, signed by President Andrew Jackson, forcibly removed Native Americans from their homes through emigration into reservations and new areas. There were at least five tribes that were affected through ethnic cleansing. The Cherokee, Chickasaw, Creek, Seminole and Choctaw were forcibly removed from their land and homes during the years of 1831-1838. The trail that was created by the emigration of these tribes became known as the "Trail of Tears." Not all were simply relocated; others lost their lives trying to defend their land, homes and families.

The result of this, as well as other injustices, has left countless families affected by generational roots of heaviness, bitterness and many generational curses that are in need of being broken.

Many people have some degree of Native American heritage in their family line, even if it is remote. Just because the physical traits may not be recognizable any more doesn't mean the spiritual ties aren't still there. As citizens of the United States, it's important for us to identify with and ask God to forgive the sin of those that pioneered and settled our cities and our nation. We must ask our Father to forgive the sins of our forefathers, our presidents and political leaders that broke treaties and treacherously removed the boundary lines of Native Americans, and impoverished them in the process. It resulted in many broken hearts and broken lives; the evidence that is still seen today. We need to acknowledge these things before God so that the guilt of these sins can be covered by the blood of Jesus. Many of the people that pioneered and settled this land, Spaniards and others, including Native Americans, brought the pagan practices, cultures and traditions brought in from foreign lands. This has left an impact in the foundations of our cities, and the familiar spirits that remain in the land to perpetuate a curse.

"A 2011 study performed by Minnesota Indian Women's Sexual Assault Coalition and the San Francisco–based Prostitution Research & Education held interviews with more than 100 Native American women. "Before this, nobody had ever done research speaking with Native American women used in prostitution and trafficking," says Nicole Matthews, executive director of the coalition.

The report found that 92 percent of the women had been raped, 84 percent were physically assaulted, and 72 percent suffered traumatic brain injuries in prostitution. Almost all the women—98 percent—were either currently or previously homeless. Seventy-nine percent of the women interviewed said they had been sexually abused as children by an average of four perpetrators.

Nearly half the women in the study had been used by more than 200 sex buyers, and 16 percent had been used by at least 900 sex buyers. At the time of their interviews, 52 percent of the women had posttraumatic-stress syndrome, a rate comparable to that of combat veterans. Seventy-one percent manifested symptoms of dissociation. "There's times I'd walk around in a space-out because when I stop and think about reality, I break down and can't handle it," one woman said.

Most of the prostitutes had sought help for their problems, with 80 percent using outpatient substance-abuse services, 77 percent using homeless shelters, 65 using domestic-violence services, and 33 percent using sexual-assault services.

Although 92 percent of the women said they wanted to escape prostitution, the study reported that "there are currently few or no available services especially designed for Native women in prostitution."

Sarah Deer, co-author of the study, says, "Over hundreds of years, Indian people were systematically stripped of their land, their language, their spirituality, and their safety." "Colonization accounts for the vulnerability of Native women, because even though a lot of these policies happened a long time ago, they still have present-day effects. It's intergenerational trauma; if your mother and grandmother and great-grandmother were all victims of sexual assault, there's a normalization of that crime in your culture, where it seems as if everyone is a victim. " [6]

Though we have no idea where the women were from, one thing is clear. These women are suffering from an unbroken generational curse that began with the history of their ancestors. If no one tells them they can break it through the power of prayer, they will continue to suffer. And, not just them, but so many other families that suffer from areas of brokenness.

No one needs to suffer when Jesus' grace, love and willingness to heal is so readily available. He longs to heal our soul and set us free! We have a responsibility to ourselves, our families and others. If we want the families in our cities to be healthy, if we want to re-write the destiny of our families, our cities, and our nation, then we cannot look upon the misery and bondage of others with casual disregard. We must labor to destroy the works of the evil one and send him back to the pit from where he came.

---

[6] Leslie Bennets, Native American Nightmare, October27, 2011, http://www.thedailybeast.com/articles/2011/10/26/native-american-women-expose-brutal-life-of-prostitution.html

CHAPTER FOUR
RESTORING FOUNDATIONS

"If the foundations are destroyed, what can the righteous do?"
Psalm 11:3

This is the taunt from the mouth of the enemy. He has long been at work attempting to destroy the foundations of our nation. It's important to realize though, that you have a personal foundation. What you build your life upon is important. The foundation of any structure is beneath the surface. It isn't seen, but it is vitally important to the rest of the building process. The foundation of our nation is based on laws and order that protect and preserve the rights of American citizens. The foundation of your home allows for the rest of the house to be built safely and provide a sound structure that can withstand natural elements such as wind, rain, and storms.

Jesus understood the importance of a spiritual foundation. He compared a wise builder to a foolish builder, illustrated in the parable about two builders. The first man was likened to a smart carpenter that built his house with the proper foundation. The second man was a foolish carpenter, who built his house upon the sand. In this story, found in Matthew 7:24-27, Jesus illustrated the difference between those who hear and apply the wisdom found in His word, and those who hear but never apply that knowledge to their lives.

I remember our years living in Florida. We had just moved there right before Hurricane Ivan hit. It just so happened that the panhandle where we lived received a great deal of damage as it was not far from the eye of the storm. The devastation from that storm was enormous. We drove out to the beach areas where it got hit the hardest to see the damage. We were utterly shocked and saddened by what we saw. Some homes and businesses looked like a huge wrecking ball had taken out parts of the buildings. It literally looked like a war zone. Certain buildings that we knew had once been in a particular location were reduced to piles of rubble, and some an empty lot. Even the foundations were gone. I remember feeling an incredible sense of awe at the immense, unbridled power of nature. I had walked those areas and been in some of those businesses just days earlier. One of the restrooms on the beach, completely made of concrete blocks was just gone, as if it had evaporated into thin air! I wondered how a storm like

Hurricane Ivan could completely remove an entire concrete structure as if it never even existed. It was an eerie feeling, but suddenly the parable of the wise builder and the foolish builder came alive before my very eyes.

We drove around and it was amazing to see how many homes had their foundations exposed. Parts of them were missing and some homes seemed to balance precariously on unstable legs. Many resembled more like a game of Jenga than homes. Walls, roofs and other parts of their structures were missing, exposing all that was in those homes. Personal belongings were scattered in the streets. That's a lesson in itself. When God allows the exterior walls of people's lives to come crashing down, everyone can see what's really on the inside. What was even more amazing to me is that after a while, some folks began the rebuilding process right in the very same spot where their homes got damaged. They were rebuilding on the same sand that washed away their foundation.

Living in an area that had hurricane season every single year, it seemed disheartening to think that inevitability the next big catastrophe lurked somewhere just around the corner. Within less than a year, Hurricane Katrina brought another devastating storm. Many people's rebuilding efforts were washed away. It struck me that people's lives often look a lot like that, too. How often do we try to build something new upon the ruins of our yesterdays, only to repeat the cycles of loss again and again?

Although I share a love for the beach communities, I wondered why anyone would foolishly try to go through the expense, time and wasted effort only to have it get washed away again. That's a lot of heartache and disappointment. Sand will always be unstable and it's just not wise to build upon something that shifts so easily. If the foundation that you can't see is prone to collapse, the devastation of the rest of the structure will topple like a house of cards. Jesus pointed out that those that hear God's warnings and wisdom but never actually apply those lessons to their lives are like the person who tried to build their house without a proper foundation. The Message Bible says it like this:

"These words I speak to you are not incidental additions to your life, homeowner improvements to your standard of living. They are foundational words, words to build a life on. If you work these words into your life, you are like a smart carpenter that built his house on solid rock. Rain poured down, the river flooded, a tornado hit - but nothing moved that house. It was fixed to the rock.

"But if you just use my words in Bible studies and don't work them into your life, you are like a stupid carpenter who built his house on the sandy beach. When a storm rolled in and the waves

came up, it collapsed like a house of cards." Matthew 7:24-27

"For no one can lay a foundation other than that which is laid, which is Jesus Christ." 1 Corinthians 3:11 ESV

In Matthew chapter 16, Jesus himself posed the question to Peter as to who Peter thought He was. Peter answered, "You are the Christ." Then Jesus announced that it would be this revelation upon which His church was built. *Revelation is a gift from God.* No one can truly enter into a relationship with God without first having the revelation of the person of Jesus Christ. Our eyes must be opened to see Him as the Holy, Anointed, Son of God. He's not just a man. He's not just a teacher, a prophet, or a person with great morals. He is God in human form that came to live among us, loving us, sharing truths about His kingdom, of which He is King. He did wonders among us, healing the sick, driving out demons from the tormented and oppressed. He was rejected, scorned, physically abused, publicly shamed, had a bounty put on his head and became a wanted man. This was His earthly reward for choosing to love greatly. His level of goodness and morality so superseded those around him that the light of His goodness and purity pierced the darkness of men's hearts. The conviction they felt was so intense that people felt exposed, vulnerable, fearful and ashamed of the darkness within them - so much so, that they couldn't wait to get rid of Him. And so they did. They falsely accused Him, deprived Him of justice, crucified Him and left Him hanging on a wooden cross. Yet, the purity of His heart continued to shine in the darkness until he exhaled His last breath.

"Father forgive them. They know not what they do." Luke 23:24.

No one in their right mind would go through all of that unless they were either out of their mind, or not of this world. Now, just as then, when people hear the story of the Gospel, they must come to a decision: Was He insane, or the Son of the Living God just as He proclaimed? **No one** sacrificially gives their life in exchange for others that would put them through that sort of hell. It takes supernatural grace, empowerment from a holy source, to live as Jesus lived. And we've only just touched on His life. We haven't even talked about His resurrection yet. You can't even explain that event outside of it witnessing to the reality and power of God. So the question to you is, who do *you* say Jesus is? Are your eyes opened to see Him for who He really is? He is standing at the door of your heart, knocking, waiting patiently for each person to open the door to Him that He may come in. If you would like to invite Jesus in, all you need to do is pray.

Holy Spirit, please open my eyes to see Jesus for who He really is. Take the veil away from my understanding and give me personal revelation. Heavenly Father, I believe Jesus is the Son

of God, and I ask You to forgive my sin. Please accept me as Your child. I thank You for sending Your Son to die in my place so that I may know You. Lord Jesus, I invite you into my heart as my Lord and Savior. Thank you for what You have done for me. Let Your Holy Spirit give me power to live for You. In Your name I pray, amen.

The revelation that everything else is built upon is Jesus Christ. He is the cornerstone of our foundation. He builds His house inside of us and comes to live within our hearts. Each one of us has been graciously invited to become a part of God's building project. All we have to do is say yes. Have you accepted God's offer of salvation? If so,

"Therefore you are no longer strangers and foreigners, but fellow citizens of the saints and members of God's household, built on the foundation of the apostles and prophets with Christ Jesus Himself being the cornerstone." Ephesians 2:20

"Because you are his sons, God sent the Spirit of his Son into our hearts, the Spirit who calls out, "Abba, Father." "So you are no longer a slave, but a son; and since you are a son, you are also an heir through God...." Galatians 4:6,7 NIV

Every outsider becomes an insider. Every sinner becomes a

saint. Every orphan becomes part of a family. Every individual becomes part of the something greater than themselves, the body of Christ. Every member of the body of Christ becomes part of the church, which is compared to a building. The building is laid upon the foundation, of which the (accurate) revelation of Christ is key. The Apostle Paul said this in 1 Corinthians 3:10:

"By the grace God has given me, as a wise master builder I have laid the foundation…"

Let us remember the importance of building on truth. Whether it concerns an individual, a family, local church, a city or our nation, the principle is the same. A foundation may not necessarily be visible but it exists. Foundations can be either shallow or deep. The words shallow and deep refer to the depth of soil in which the foundation is made.[7] Spiritual foundations are built upon belief systems. Beliefs shape people's heart, character and actions. Actions are the fruit of character, and just as people are known by their fruit of their actions, so are cities. So is our nation.

Every city has a character and is known for attributes that reflect the character of those living there. It can either reflect sin,

---

[7] Understanding Construction, http://www.understandconstruction.com/types-of-foundations.html

or righteousness. It can reflect good character, or bad character. The question to every person reading this is, "How do people know you? Other people see us differently than we see ourselves. What do you think they feel when they see you? You become a part of what is reflected to others. What do you want your city to be known for?"

You can see by this illustration the importance of a sound foundation. One of the ways Jesus builds a sound foundation in us is through His word. His word is not just text on a page, but it is described as living, active, and contains the power to change the human heart. The word of God leaves an impression on people. The mind ponders, analyzes and digests what it has read, but the devil is very diligent in his efforts to send distractions and deter people away from the truth. In this way, the word of God cannot leave a lasting impression upon the mind. The mind represents shallow soil, and thus produces a shallow foundation. The mind alone cannot produce the change that is needed in the person's internal structure. The person never really experiences a depth of growth in character, and the fruit of their actions reflect what they believe about themselves and others.

If the mind *retains* the words of God and the devil doesn't come to steal them away, they actually have a chance to sink into the person's heart. The heart can represent deeper soil and a deeper foundation. The human heart may also represent hard ground, where the seeds of the word of God have a hard time growing. Holy Spirit works on the individual to try to soften their heart so that the word of God can sink in even deeper. Genuine change is produced in the human heart. That can only occur when something in the person's foundation, or their personal belief system, changes. Some life experiences change a person's heart for the worse; some for the better. We all have flaws and weaknesses in our foundation. God may need to take a spiritual jackhammer to our foundation and dig it up before He can pour a new one. If we remain moldable in His hands, He will pour in His love, mercy and truth. This is what helps to form a new, stronger, stable foundation that is rooted and grounded in bedrock. It becomes the anchor to our soul. When we build our lives upon the foundation of Jesus Christ, storms may come and go, but we will not be shaken.

The enemy wants to destroy our godly foundations. He is always asking the question, "If the foundation is destroyed, what *will* you do?" He knows how significant they are, but we have failed to recognize this truth. God's people are called to restore the foundations that have been broken down.

"Those from among you will rebuild the ancient ruins; You will raise up the age-old foundations; And you will be called the repairer of the breach, The restorer of the streets in which to

dwell." Isaiah 58:12 Berean Study Bible

"Then they will rebuild the ancient ruins, They will raise up the former devastations; And they will repair the ruined cities, The desolations of many generations." Isaiah 61:4

If we understood the significance of what the enemy is attempting to do by stealing our foundations, we would not cooperate with his schemes. We would stand up to those that are attempting to take us into captivity through their puffed up, self-aggrandizing philosophies.

The Pharisees of today look much different than those of our past. The Pharisaical spirit of biblical times represented a strict adherence to the law. They utilized shaming, intimidation, rejection and an endless amount of rules and regulations to support their man made traditions and religious beliefs. They forced their will upon others in order to try to control them and trouble them into subjection. This is essentially witchcraft. Witchcraft forces the will of one person onto others without their consent. Witchcraft and control do exist in the church, but they also exist in politics and government as well. Jesus warned us to beware of the leaven of the Pharisees and Sadducees. These were two different groups of religious leaders. He likened destructive doctrines to making bread, comparing these destructive doctrines and beliefs to yeast that would permeate the whole lump of dough.[8] The Book of Colossians also issues a warning that we don't allow ourselves to be taken into captivity through worldly philosophies and beliefs that hinder faith.

"Take care lest there be someone who leads you away as prisoners by means of his philosophy and idle fancies, following human traditions and the world's crude notions instead of following Christ." Colossians 2:8, Weymouth New Testament

The convictions of progressivism and political beliefs tied into socialism are, for the most part, the destructive doctrines of today. The invasive laws and regulations behind the belief systems of these convictions have systematically infringed upon the basic rights and privileges afforded to us by God; slowly and methodically taking our dreams into captivity and squelching our creativity. It is time for us to dream again, and be willing to do what is necessary to engage with God to bring our hopes, dreams and the future of our families out of captivity. These empty philosophies, like the leaven of the Pharisees and Sadducees, has permeated every part of our whole nation. Ideologies that promise what they can't deliver are void of the wisdom, conviction and morality of God. The promise of a better future to a nation of

---

[8] Matthew 6:16, The NIV Study Bible ©1995, Zondervan Publishing House

people who were tired of feeling like they were losing offered hope, but many put their trust in empty inflated promises that caused them to experience even more disappointment and bondage. People have been anesthetized into a twilight sleep because they took the bait -- hook, line and sinker. Progressivism is a philosophy while socialism is a political definition, but both are based on an impractical world view. The perception created, and the lies that are spun, are aimed at convincing people that everyone will benefit and be better off in a political system that convinces people to let the government be their parents and providers. It's all just an illusion.

How do you keep people dependent? Offer what they feel they cannot do without or achieve by any other means, then threaten to take those benefits away if they fail to comply with every little rule and regulation. This is a poverty system designed to keep people dependent upon the government; therefore government becomes a replacement for God. When people lean more on the government to take care of them than they lean on God, then it can be very easy to have misplaced trust. We must be very careful not to break faith with our heavenly Father. This is why it is so dangerous to give away our God-given dominion. If you give it away, others will gladly (and predictably) abuse that power.

These political philosophies really are the religion of those swept away by worldly influences, because to them it has become the code of ethics and morality by which they live. They've exchanged the beliefs, moral customs and wisdom found in God's word for empty philosophies of progressivism and other man-made ontology. It's obvious by the state of our world these destructive ideologies do not actually deliver what they promise. Man's wisdom will never be superior to God's wisdom. People have placed their faith in world leaders and government programs to provide for them, rather than putting their trust in the Lord. As a nation of people, many people have traded God in for something that sounded like a better idea, but people didn't realize they made a god of their own understanding.

"These people have exchanged God's truth for a lie. So they have become ungodly and serve what is created rather than the Creator, who is blessed forever. Amen!" Romans 1:25, God's Word Translation

Foundations are based on history, law, order and beliefs. In order to destroy our beliefs, we must first lose our sense of who we are and where we came from. When a nation forgets its history, it loses its identity. We see so much media bias and censorship that is nothing more than an attempt to shelter people from the truth. The censorship is there to help shape a perception and world view based on incomplete information. Incomplete information means people lack the facts and understanding that if they knew what was being withheld from them, they would probably reach a very different conclusion. It is the enemy's attempt to not only steal truth and hide the facts, but also reshape history through the ways people remember certain events. We also see this taking place in our children's history books. A great deal of Christian history is being omitted in the newer books, and more about other religions is being included. Little by little, Christianity is being written out of historical events.

Consider what is written by journalist Carly Hill, in an online article titled, *High School Text Book Literally Re-Writes History.*[9] Hill takes note of a news piece featured on the Todd Starnes news program. What caused a sense of alarm in many parents is the fact that their teens history books, a Prentiss Hall World History text book, completely *re-wrote* certain aspects of historical events and omitted others altogether.

Some people are no longer here to tell their story, but their stories are still important. We must honor them and remember what part their lives have had in history. People like Harriet

---

[9] Hill: *High School Text Book Literally Re-Writes History*, July 31, 2013, GenFringe.com; http://genfringe.com/2013/07/high-school-text-book-literally-re-writes-history/

Tubman, who helped lead blacks out of slavery, and Rosa Parks, who was a social activist for equal rights, were freedom fighters and advocates of social equality. Their lives played an important part in history and their stories are vital not just to black history, but American history. Others, such as Corrie Ten Boom and Doris Martin, have told their horrendous stories of suffering in German concentration camps, surviving the Nazi Holocaust. They are just a few. Should their stories be wiped out by those who wish to portray a different version of historical facts? The younger generations are vulnerable in the fact that they must trust the older generations to give them an accurate, unbiased perspective of historical events. Each person is a testimony of historical information, whether they are alive or not. It's important to keep telling their stories. We cannot afford to let the enemy paint a different picture than what really happened. He doesn't get off the hook that easily. We are compelled by the Lord Himself to forgive the past and those the enemy used to carry out evil, but God help us; don't let it be wiped away as though it never happened! If we don't learn from our history we will be forced to repeat it.

The history of a nation is what binds us together. We use technology that was invented long before our time. We live in a society long established with certain beliefs that help us hold on to our humanity. There are so many complexities and traditions of our culture that shape who we are; it gives us a sense of belonging.

History gives us roots. On the other hand, people without a sense of home, family and belonging become unstable wanderers. They feel no sense of commitment or loyalty to anyone other than themselves. They don't prove to be productive members of society. They become troubled with a sense of feeling fatherless, abandoned and have difficulty navigating through life. This is what many people are suffering from today. They are failing to thrive because of a spirit of abandonment and fatherlessness. They have no sense of foundation and no ability to really build their lives. God wants us rooted in Him. There is a fatherless generation crying out in pain, but if we take the love of the father to them, He will touch them once again. If we will simply show the love of the Father, He will break the chains that bind them and heal their wounds.

Builders, *build.* There are many people that are not builders however; they are partners with the destroyer because their only plan is to destroy and tear down. These are people who are leading others into disrespecting the inheritance that we've been given by God. They profess to care about social justice issues, but they do not care where this nation is headed. They incite anger, divisiveness and violence but do not take responsibility for their actions or their words. They are committed to tearing down anything that is built or established by God, anything that represents family values or Christian beliefs. They want to re-write history to eliminate our God-given freedoms, and they don't want to take responsibility for the stewardship of this godly inheritance that has been given to us. These people want to remove the beliefs, morals, values and identity that represents who we are as a nation so that they can do what is right in their own eyes.

The destroyer wants to remove our constitution and enact a new one; leading people further away from God, because by doing so he gains legal grounds to enforce the curse upon us. He wants to be god over this nation and over our families. Satan looks for any way possible to entice us into agreement with him. Through deceptive and destructive philosophies, we give away our dominion and exchange freedoms for captivity.

Those that spread propaganda and share these destructive doctrines and philosophies are attempting to tear up this nation's foundation and lay down a new one. These 'voices' use fear, bullying and coercion to intimidate people into submission. This is why the spirit of witchcraft and rebellion are so strong. We put people in office that had that same spirit. This is the enemy's attempt to steal our identity and re-create us in his image. If Satan can effectively steal away the knowledge that *we have been created in God's image* **to exercise dominion over him**, then he can steal our identity. When a nation loses its history, it loses its identity. When a nation loses its identity, the people lose their democracy, freedom and justice.

Alexis De Tocqueville was a 19th century French diplomat, political scientist and historian. He was probably also a prophetic voice long before his time. "In his work, *"Democracy in America,"* De Tocqueville analyzed living standards and social conditions of individuals, as well as their relationship to the market and state in Western societies. Tocqueville wrote of the New World and its burgeoning democratic order. He saw democracy as a balance between liberty and equality, showing concern for the individual as well as the community. Tocqueville was an ardent supporter of liberty. "I have a passionate love for liberty, law, and respect for rights", he wrote. "I am neither of the revolutionary party nor of the conservative....Liberty is my foremost passion." [10]

"Tocqueville warned that modern democracy may be adept at inventing new forms of tyranny, because radical equality could lead to the materialism of an expanding bourgeoisie and to the selfishness of individualism. In such conditions we lose interest in the future of our descendants...and meekly allow ourselves to be led in ignorance by a despotic force all the more powerful because

---

[10] de Tocqueville, Alexis (1835). De la démocratie en Amérique. I (1 ed.). Paris: Librairie de Charles Gosselin. Retrieved 24 June 2015. via Gallica

it does not resemble one." [11]

"Tocqueville worried that if despotism were to take root in a modern democracy, it would be a much more dangerous version than the oppression under the Roman emperors or tyrants of the past who could only exert a pernicious influence on a small group of people at a time."

"In contrast, a despotism under a democracy could see "a multitude of men", uniformly alike, equal, "constantly circling for petty pleasures", unaware of fellow citizens, and subject to the will of a powerful state which exerted an "immense protective power". Tocqueville compared a potentially despotic democratic government to a protective parent who wants to keep its citizens (children) as "perpetual children", and which doesn't break men's wills but rather guides it, and presides over people in the same way as a shepherd looking after a "flock of timid animals." [12]

Sound familiar? We've heard a great deal of this from certain political leaders. This is what we continually hear from people

---

[11] James, "Tocqueville In America", The New Yorker, 17 May 2010.

[12] Joshua Kaplan (2005). "Political Theory: The Classic Texts and their Continuing Relevance". The Modern Scholar. 14 lectures; (lectures #11 & #12) – see disc 6

with a god complex; leaders that seek to be 'like God,' ruling over us as though we were children incapable of making our own decisions. They believe they have a right to take away our right to choice. The so-called 'welfare' of the majority trumps the rights of the individual, and thus, individual civil rights are gradually removed. Government policies, laws and regulations have progressively moved to undermine the family unit and redefine the order established by God. Government policies, laws and regulations have been established that redefine a person's gender, the marriage union and even the right to life. These are destructive ideologies that remove moral absolutes and replaces them with subjective personal preference. This is another tactic of the enemy to strip us of the identity given to us by God, and recreate a false identity. Satan is determined to re-create people in *his* image; the image of perversion and immorality. Confusion brings disorder. Neither are of God, nor should they become the accepted norm for any society.

Tyranny is disguised as a philosophy of progressivism. This philosophy is about embarrassment and shaming, forcing people who dare to disagree into places of hiddenness. These tyrannical voices insist that Christians come under the thumb of government control in order to intimidate them into silence. It's time to recover our voice and pray for God to protect our freedoms and constitutional rights, preserve our godly inheritance and restore the foundation of our nation. The strength of our nation is our families.

* * *

There is another era of history that is rapidly being forgotten by Americans. "The 1965 Voting Acts Right restored African-Americans to full citizenship in the United States after a century of legalized oppression. As the era fades deeper and deeper into the past, Americans are rapidly forgetting the historical realities of Jim Crow." [13]

Jim Crow was a way of life in the southern and border states established by white elitists designed to oppress blacks. Black people were seen as inferior and unequal to whites and often treated with cruelty as a subhuman race. The principles of black inferiority pervaded every aspect of life.

When the Civil War ended in 1865, slavery ended also, but the prejudices, bigotry and injustices still infiltrated the belief systems of those affected by this period in American life. "Blacks began to campaign for equal rights, including the right to vote. Democratic President Andrew Johnson allowed southern states to implement

---

[13] *"The Truth About Jim Crow,"* ©2014; American Civil Rights Union, pgs. 4,5; http://www.theacru.org/jimcrow/

certain 'black codes' that restricted and controlled the newly freed slaves." (*The Truth About Jim Crow*, ©2014 ACRU).

The 1866 Congressional elections brought a turning of the tide, as the Republicans gained control. The Republicans began to fight to restore the full rights of citizenship of the blacks, and the Republican party successfully engineered the 14th and 15th amendments, which extended equal protection of laws to former slaves, and also guaranteed their right to vote. Because southern states had substantial black populations, black candidates began to win local and state elections." The black population of voters dramatically increased the size and influence of the Republican party. Blacks were at that time, primarily Republican.

The growth of black political power and social status became a threat to whites, and hostility grew. The white elitists in the Democratic party were afraid of losing their power. Many political moves were made between the parties, negotiating the tradeoff of power and influence. "The Democrats at that time controlled the House of Representatives, which allowed them to prevent the inauguration of a new president. So, they made a trade. They allowed a Republican president, Rutherford B. Hayes, to get into the White House, in exchange for the withdrawal of Federal troops still occupying the south. When the troops left, the south was left in the hands of the Democratic Party." The Democratic Party has always considered itself to be the 'party of the white man..' They started passing laws throughout the region, bringing blacks back under oppressive government control, asserting white supremacy by passing laws that infringed upon the rights of blacks and enforced strict segregation." [14]

Part of these oppressive laws were voter denial. It was the only way the Democratic Party could try to regain control of their political power and influence. They strove to maintain white political dominance at any cost. "Poll taxes were implemented, which drastically reduced the amount of people who could afford to vote. If blacks tried to vote, they were threatened, beaten and killed. Some had their homes or farms burned down. Some lost their jobs and had their family members harmed."[15] "Jim Crow laws were an entire complex system devoted to injustice and oppression of blacks. These laws were designed to deny African-Americans (and sometimes Latinos and Native Americans) civil rights, voting rights, and the ability to be treated with equity."[16]

---

[14] *The Truth About Jim Crow*, ©2014; ACRU, pg. 5;
http://www.theacru.org/wordpress/wp-content/uploads/2015/02/ACRU-the-truth-about-jim-crow_v2.pdf

[15] *The Truth About Jim Crow*, ©2014; ACRU, pgs. 8,9;
http://www.theacru.org/wordpress/wp-content/uploads/2015/02/ACRU-the-truth-about-jim-crow_v2.pdf

[16] Crow, ©2014. ACRU, pg.9; http://www.theacru.org/wordpress/wp-

White supremacists were responsible for an incredible amount of injustice, bigotry and hatred. Looking back, the tremendous injustices done toward African-Americans seems like it was less about skin color as it was about holding on to political power. The ugliness of racism made it about color, but in many ways it was much more about who would wield power and control.

Lynching was seen as an effective means of intimidation and control over the black people. Many of them were done in broad daylight in the middle of public squares. These are key areas in our cities where prophetic acts of healing and reconciliation can prove to release healing to the land. We must utterly destroy racial hatred, divisiveness and bitterness that were the result of tremendous injustice. We must take responsibility for the pain that was caused to so many people.

It has been 50 years since these laws were in effect. An entire generation has grown up in the absence of these terrible restrictions that were placed upon the African-American community. Most people in this current generation would probably not even know what the Jim Crow laws were about. Yet, the racial prejudice, divisiveness, hatred, anger and bitterness over injustices done by past generations still lingers. **When** will it stop? Only when people

---

content/uploads/2015/02/ACRU-the-truth-about-jim-crow_v2.pdf

make a conscious decision to address it God's way. That bitter root must be pulled up and out of the land. We must want a better future for our children and grandchildren and refuse to perpetuate the anger and bitterness. Our children must know what God expects of them, and He holds us accountable for giving them instruction. We must give them a proper example of living out forgiveness. We must make the choice to receive our own healing before we can expect others to change. Healing comes from forgiveness. *Forgiveness robs the enemy of his power.* When we retain unforgiveness, we give away our power and put it in the hands of those that do not care about our pain. Holding on to anger and bitterness exalts the very enemy that despises us, in a position of control over us. The enemy becomes managers of our emotions, our pain, our future. God gives each person a destiny consistent with their choices. Isn't it time to take back your power and your greatness? The question presented to each person is, **"Are you strong enough to forgive?"**

In many cities, the division between whites and blacks and the racial hatred has been rekindled because the root of bitterness has never been healed. Bitterness wants war. There is a root of war in this nation that must be destroyed. If we don't eradicate the works of the evil one, the destroyer will destroy us. Again, it comes down to what foundation we choose to build upon. We can build our lives upon bitterness, anger, strife and war. We can let gangs, turf wars, addictions, prostitution, generational poverty, drug lords and violence overtake our land and push us out of our inheritance. Or, we can have our eyes opened to the enemy's game and refuse to play. We can take the power out of the enemy's hands by renouncing the sins of generations past, cleanse our bloodline through the blood of Jesus, and cleanse our consciences from the guilt and shame of knowing that our hearts have not been right with God and others.

For the sake of our families and future generations, we must think of how our attitudes and actions will serve to either cut off the generational curse of bitterness, racism, anger and poverty; or we can do nothing and let another generation go by, dealing with the same pain, the same short sightedness and bigotry that exists today. I pray that together, within our cites and in our nation, we can forgive the past and move forward. Let us heal the broken foundation and shore up the cracks. The enemy is betting on the fact that we won't do it. I pray we can prove him wrong.

During the years we lived in Florida, we held a couple of multi-church gatherings in outdoor parks. We called them "A Heart for the City," events because God has such great love and compassion for His cities. We did not realize the significance of the first one until later, but it was held in the very same park where there had been a public lynching in 1908.[17] One hundred years later, we held an outreach aimed at healing and reconciling relationships that had been broken. We repented for sins committed in the city, both current and past sins of generations that came before us. We prayed for peace, unity and restoration. The sins of the past needed to be acknowledged so they could be forgiven and covered by the blood of Jesus.

During that outreach, we fed the homeless, offered a variety of different services to the general public and we also invited people from the gathering to come pray for the healing and reconciliation of relationships. There were so many miracles that took place that day. We spontaneously invited some local pastors to come up to the stage and pray for healing among the pastors of the city. What we did not realize until after it was over was two of the pastors on stage had been involved in a church split and had not talked to one another since it happened. That day it was put under the blood of Jesus. Sometimes those situations feel awkward and uncomfortable, but they are so necessary. Forgiveness and healing comes when people are ready to respond to one another with humility and kindness. It's not about rehashing the past or Lording

---

[17] Scott Satterwhite and Duwayne Escobedo, *"Lillie and Leander: A Legacy of Violence" Vol. 8, No. 16, April 19, 2007;* Independent News, http://inweekly.net/article.asp?artID=4410

over others with our complaints or demands; it's about extending grace to others and letting it go. Healing doesn't come any other way. The same way we heal relationships between individuals can help heal the heart of our cities. *Heal the cities, heal the nation.*

We saw many miracles that day. A couple months later a 40 day prayer and fasting campaign was held by Joe Miller, a local businessman and leader of the prayer movement. Miller was an ordinary guy with a heart for his city, and his passion helped to create a momentum that is still being felt today. The first year of the prayer movement was an election year. God really cleaned house that year in the local city elections. The old order was swept out and new people came in. At Joe's request, I wrote a spiritual Declaration of Independence modeled after the original Declaration. It was read aloud at the final worship gathering celebration. We came into agreement with a new declaration of faith over the city and spoke a blessing over it. Many of the local pastors came up and signed it after the celebration, and we had it framed. We later presented it to the Mayor of Pensacola at a City Council Meeting. Every year since then the Pray for Pensacola prayer team, headed up by Joe and Karina Miller, enlists the aid of regular citizens that have a desire to change their city. It involves pastors, worship leaders, prayer warriors, stay-at-home moms, bankers, politicians, businessmen and women, and some tougher-than-nails little grey haired grandmas that can pull heaven down to earth. Don't mess with the grandmas! Those ladies know how to pray! Ordinary people can accomplish extraordinary things when they work together in unity. When God can find people to work together in unity, He pours out His anointing to bring breakthrough.

CHAPTER FIVE
DEMONIC FOUNDATIONS

"Shout against her round about: she hath given her hand: her foundations are fallen, her walls are thrown down: for it is the vengeance of the LORD: take vengeance upon her; as she hath done, do unto her." Jeremiah 50:15 KJV

Understanding personal foundations is important, but so is understanding the nature of spiritual foundations that have been laid in a city. Before an altar can be built, there has to first be a foundation. Once a foundation has been built, an altar can be activated. Altars are portals, or doorways, into the spiritual realm, where either good or evil comes through. Foundations are where the enemy hides himself. Foundations, altars, doors and gates are all access points; therefore we must learn to discern what they are and how they work.

It was said of Abraham that *"he looked forward to a city with eternal foundations, a city designed and built by God."* Hebrews 11:10, NLT.

God loves His cities. Father has a plan, a purpose and a calling for each city. In order to understand this we need to look to Revelation chapter 21 and 22. These chapters describe a holy city that is no longer plagued by sin, prepared for the bride of Christ. The Apostle John describes the holy city as coming down out of heaven like a bride adorned for her husband. The imagery depicts the place where the 'church' is prepared for 'the marriage.' John saw the beauty of its existence, and we know by faith that the New Holy City exists in the spiritual realm. John saw the New Jerusalem coming down in a manner that essentially superimposed itself upon the earth, but the earth as we know it today had passed away; even the sea was no more. The city was renewed in every way. This reveals God's ultimate plan and purpose for every city. The New Jerusalem is a pattern and blueprint for renewal, restoration, and a return to purity. In the New Jerusalem there is no stain of sin, bondage or demonic oppression. Every area that was once a part of Satan's domain (the earth as we know it now) will be redeemed out of the hand of the wicked oppressor.

When Lucifer was deposed from his position in heaven and cast to the earth, the earth became his domain. This occurred even before Adam and Eve were formed, because the adversary took the form of a serpent in the Garden of Eden. Jesus said of him in Luke 10:18, *"I saw Satan fall like lightning from heaven."* The word of God (Jesus) was with God in the beginning, from before time began, and He witnessed Satan falling like lightning, forever banned from being welcomed in the presence of God.

The earth became Satan's domain, though it would be on a temporary basis. In Luke 4:5,6 Satan tempted Jesus by offering him the kingdoms of the earth if he would worship him.

"Then the devil, taking him up on a high mountain, showed Him all the kingdoms of the world in a moment of time. And the devil said to Him, 'All this authority I will give You, and their glory; for this had been delivered to me, and I give it to whomever I wish."

Later in John 12:31, Jesus referred to Satan as the ruler of this world.

"The time for judging this world has come, when Satan, the ruler of this world, will be cast out." NLT

Satan's permanent eternal dwelling will one day be the lake of fire. But, until then, there is a war over who will ultimately take dominion over the earth.

The New Jerusalem shows us a picture of God's ultimate goal for our cities. His desire is for a people who will prepare their hearts and lives for His coming by ridding themselves from the stain of sin. Only His blood can redeem us and cleanse us from sin. He is looking for a people who will pursue His presence, cooperate with Him in self-deliverance, and earnestly desire the restoration of purity in their lives.

All of these things seem impossible to achieve, and they would be unless He provided the ability to do it. If we stop to think about the impossibility of entire cities turning to God, revival taking over our nation…well, it seems quite an overwhelming task. But we aren't trying to do it in our own strength. We serve a God that loves to work in ways we cannot possible imagine, and He supplies the ability to get the job done.

"The things that are impossible with men are possible with God." Luke 18:27

"For with God, nothing shall be impossible." Luke 1:37

Understanding God's purpose for mankind and his cities also helps us understand why Satan would go to extreme lengths to try to prevent God's plans from coming to pass. Every day we come closer to the appearance of the New Jerusalem is one day closer to

Satan's eternal punishment in the lake of fire. He is full of fear knowing that his time is shorter now than ever. He has been waging war against the children of God for thousands of years, and he has had plenty of time to formulate his plans to try to deceive, scheme and plot against God's people.

Satan understands the importance of blueprints and how cities fit into God's ultimate plan. He has an authority structure and hierarchy in the kingdom of darkness. Satan has gone to great lengths to incorporate his influence in the very early foundations of our cities and upon our nation. It is no wonder that our capital city was one of the earliest cities mapped out by the enemy. Whoever controls the capital city controls the whole country. The mountains of pride, occult power, rebellion and defiance are no match for our God. He can send a fire to consume the mountains all the way down to their foundations. Did you know that when God addresses the mountains of opposition and their foundations, they actually hear and have to obey? It's true. Every single thing on earth must obey the word of God.

*"**Hear,** you mountains, the LORD's accusation; **listen,** you everlasting foundations of the earth. For the LORD has a case against his people; he is lodging a charge against Israel." Micah 6:2*

Foundations of cities have primarily been laid by masons, who were bricklayers, many of whom belonged to a secret society known as the Freemasons.

Freemasonry has the outward appearance of being a morally acceptable organization. It promotes loyalty, brotherhood, charitable works and moral rectitude. It appears to be simply a fraternity of sorts or a club where members focus on charitable acts as a means to redeem the inner man. It has the appearance of good, while the members pledge their loyalty and their allegiance to a false god called the Great Architect of the Universe. It is a somewhat vague, generic term representing a counterfeit substitute for the One true God, Jesus Christ. Masons also believe that their own good works are sufficient as a means of earning salvation. A person becomes their own god in search of enlightenment. These beliefs are dangerous and destructive, adamantly opposed to biblical truth, creating spiritual blindness while pledging one's soul to the devil.

In the Masonic Handbook Series by J.S.M Ward, the author offers explanation of apprentice rituals. The introduction page states quite clearly, "Do what thou will shall be the whole of the law." Well known Satanist Aleister Crowley and denounced as 'the wickedest man in the world,' founded the religion Thelema. He declared that his followers should adhere to the code of 'Do what thou wilt,' and seek to align themselves with their will through the practice of magic. (Crowley: *The Book of the Law*).

"This is what the Freemason Manly P. Hall, who Masons highly regard as a modern day Masonic philosopher revealed about Masonry's deception: Freemasonry is a fraternity within a fraternity - an outer organization concealing an inner brotherhood of the elect."

"Freemasonry is a hidden fraternal order, and defined by them as a system of morality. The first three steps are the Blue Lodge. The first degree is called Entered Apprentice. The second degree is called Fellow Craft. The Third degree is called Master Mason. Most men only go to the third degree, but if one chooses, he may advance either through the York Rite or the Scottish Rite. The Scottish Rite has thirty-two degrees. In each degree, the Mason pledges himself to a different Egyptian deity. There is a thirty-third degree that is largely honorary, but the thirty-two degrees give you access to becoming a Shriner. As a Shriner you will place your hand on the pagan Muslim Qur'an (Koran) and pledge yourself to the pagan "god" Allah."[18]

---

[18] Ward: Masonic Handbook Series, , Celephais Press, http://www.themasonictrowel.com/ebooks/freemasonry/eb0321.pdf

The greatest deceptions are surrounded by truth, in hopes that the truth overshadows the lie. Yet, even though something may appear as *mostly* good or true, the other small percentage that is intended to deceive is still a falsehood. Nothing is going to make a lie anything but a lie. That is essentially how the secret society of the Freemasons are able to deceive others. Truth is introduced along with deception, and the secret works of evil are overlooked. A lie becomes believable and accepted because they are shrouded in good works. What appears to be innocent or honorable efforts towards self-improvements allows the hidden agenda to carry on unnoticed. Many lower level members of the Masonic Lodge are not privy to certain information until they rise up in the ranks. This permits them to become sufficiently deceived until their minds are darkened by sin. Interestingly, most false religions and secret societies call this process 'enlightenment.'

Members of these cultish organizations must take oaths to pledge their allegiance to Satan. They would probably never admit this of course, as they profess to worship the Great Architect of the Universe, and present their false god in such a way that it might make a person think they were talking about our Creator and Heavenly Father. The use of Judeo Christian symbolism, Biblical references and language that sounds spiritual is simply a Trojan Horse, a cloak for deception.

The details of indoctrination, rituals and practices of Freemasons and how they are tied together with the occult could fill many books. It is not my intention to go into that sort of detail, but to sufficiently expose the deception and the connection to occult practices so that the reader gains understanding. It's been said that Satan does not have to do anything to demand worship or allegiance to him; he only needs to sufficiently distract people with deception so that they do not follow Jesus Christ. The Bible explicitly warns us of anti-Christ deceivers.

"For many deceivers have gone out into the world who do not confess Jesus Christ as coming in the flesh. This is a deceiver and an anti-Christ. Look to yourselves that we do not lose those things we worked for, but that we may receive a full reward. Whoever transgresses and does not abide in the doctrine of Christ does not have God. He who abides in the doctrine of Christ has both the Father and the Son. If anyone comes to you and does not bring this doctrine, do not receive him into your house nor greet him; for he who greets him shares in his evil deeds." 2 John 7-10.

Former United States President Harry S. Truman wrote these words as an introduction to a book called 10,000 Famous Masons by William Denslow: "We know that research is the most important step in the study of history. Comprehensive and accurate information must be available for those who would interpret trends in world happenings. History is made by men. It is therefore necessary to know about the men who have made history. In the study of the past we must know the motives that inspired men who made history. Events and dates are of no value unless we can discover what caused those events at the dates stated in what passes for history."[19] – Truman, Past Master, Missouri Lodge of Research, December 9, 1957. Truman was also a member of a secret society, The Freemasons.

Why is it important to know about the occult ties to Freemasonry? **Every city has a spiritual foundation**. There are seven mountains of influence that affect society in our world today: Religion, Family, Education, Government, Media, Arts & Entertainment, and Business. **Every mountain of influence has a foundation.** If we want to purify the influence of those mountains then we must target our prayers at the foundations of those involved in those industries. Each one of these 'mountains' exist in various places in our cities and nation. We need to pray that the convictions of those that make up the mountains of influence in our world would align with God's will and His belief system.

Satan hatched a well laid plan hundreds, if not thousands, of

---

[19] Truman, from the forward in 10,000 Famous Masons by William R. Denslow, Volume 1 A-D, © 1957.

years ago to lay his demonic symbolism into our cities, knowing that by the time we figured it out, the damage would already be done. To an occultist, certain symbols contain a hidden meaning. Some are used as a means of marking a particular territory. It's essentially an act of claiming ground for Satan. Just as a cross on a church would indicate a place where Christians gather to pray, in the same manner, certain occult symbols also depict whose territory that symbol is in, and who or what is worshipped. Whatever spirit is being summoned and enthroned will be the dominant power in that particular place.

Satan is the one who is behind greed, lust for power and corruption. The Freemasons are intricately involved with another secret society known as the Illuminati, who secretly control many aspects of society and government, and are working to establish the New World Order.

The majority of people are probably not aware of the fact that Freemasons encoded demonic symbolism into the actual street layout of various cities. For instance, if you look at an aerial view of the capital city of Washington, D.C. one can see that the street diagrams form the shapes of the central Masonic symbols: The square, compass, the rule, and the pentagram. On top of the White

House sits an inverted pentagram.[20] The Masons essentially laid the cornerstone of this nation upon a demonic order. Even the Great Seal of the United States is a mixture of Judeo-Masonic symbolism, as if somehow incorporating Judeo-Christian symbolism and beliefs and laying them next to one another would help cover the intent of the false beliefs and demonic symbolism right next to them. People have looked at those symbols for so long that they are now just accepted, familiar symbols that represent our national symbols and icons.

Subsequently, most people don't stop to think twice. They have accepted all the represented symbols as those representing the seat of our government. Yet the truth is, the Masonic symbols laid the foundational national symbols even though what they represent is allegiance to false gods and a demonic authority structure, interwoven among our own government system. Masons also conduct symbolic cornerstone building dedications on school buildings, public structures or places of worship.[21] In the consecration ceremony an invocation takes place, summoning a false god known as the Great Architect of the Universe. The words

---

[20] Barbara Aho, *"The Masonic Foundations of the United States",* Watch Unto Prayer; https://watch.pair.com/mason.html

[21] Guide to Cornerstone Laying, Copyrighted © 1999 - 2015   Phoenix Masonry, Inc., Phoenix Masonry Masonic Museum, http://www.phoenixmasonry.org/masonicmuseum/cornerstone_laying.htm

that are used almost sound like something you would hear in a religious church ceremony. They incorporate words that sound like a sanctified blessing. It even sounds like the words that are spoken are directed to God, but they are not. The offerings, the praise, the glory, is all directed to a somewhat vague, counterfeit false god known as the Great Architect of the Universe. Where are offerings, praise and worship offered? *On an altar.* Who is enthroned? Satan. Satan is behind every idol and false god.

"Christians have been led to believe that the government of the United States of America is based on the basic principles of Christian morality, which have their origin in the scriptures. Notable for propagating this misinformation are D. James Kennedy, author of a book promoting astrology, and Peter Marshall, Jr. (son of the late U.S. Senate Chaplain) who wrote *The Light and The Glory.* However, both of these ministers are members of the Council for National Policy, a secret organization founded by the globalist Council on Foreign Relations which has an anti-Christian agenda. Historical evidence militates against the view that those who formulated the fundamental documents of American government were Christians. To the contrary, not a few who wrote and signed the Declaration of Independence the Articles of Confederation and the U.S. Constitution were Diests, Theists, and Freemasons." [22]

George Washington was a member of a Virginian lodge, and a portrait from 1870 depicts Washington as the Grand Master of his lodge. [23] Of the 56 signers of the Declaration of Independence, only 9 can be listed as proof of their membership in the Masonic Lodges. They were: 1) William Ellery, an influential member of the Continental Congress and a signer of the Articles of Confederation; 2) Benjamin Franklin, who was heavily involved in politics, was also a philosopher, author and scientist. He was a member of the second Continental Congress as well as on the committee to draft the Declaration, but he was also Grand Master of his lodge in Philadelphia. 3) John Hancock, the first signer of the Declaration as well as Major General of the American Revolution became a Freemason in 1762. 4) Joseph Hewes (or Howes), was the first unofficial secretary of the Navy and a delegate to Congress in 1776. He was buried with Masonic honors at a funeral attended by George Washington. 5) William Hooper, another signer of the Declaration, was also elected to Continental Congress in 1774 and a member of the Hanover Lodge in

---

[22] Barbara Aho, "The Masonic Foundations of the United States", Watch Unto Prayer; https://watch.pair.com/mason.html

[23] Wikipedia, the Free Encyclopedia, Freemasonry, https://en.wikipedia.org/wiki/Freemasonry

Masonborough, North Carolina. 6) Robert Treat Paine, was a Massachusetts Lawyer, politician, speaker of the House of Representatives in 1777 and later, Attorney General of his state. He was a member of the Massachusetts Grand Lodge. 7) Richard Stockton, a charter master of St. John's Lodge at Princeton, earned a reputation in the legal field and later became a supreme court judge of New Jersey in 1774. 8) George Walton was a signer of the Declaration as well as the Articles of Confederation. He was also a Revolutionary War officer, a Governor of Georgia, a Chief Justice of Georgia and U.S. Senator. 9) William Whipple was a delegate to the Continental Congress, a brigadier general and went on to be the state supervisor of finances from 1782-84. Whipple was a member of St. John's Lodge in Portsmouth, New Hampshire. [24]

I believe there *were* Christians that influenced the founding of this nation, but I don't disagree that there were undoubtedly others with a mixture of beliefs. Throughout history, even today the Freemasons have included many of our nation's forefathers, military leaders, politicians, presidents and others in prominent positions. The Freemasons have also included less recognized, ordinary men that have still held a very significant role in laying

---

[24] William R. Denslow, 10,000 Famous Freemasons, © 1957 by Macoy Publishing; also *"United States Masonic Founding Fathers"* ©2016, http://freemasoninformation.com/masonic-education/famous/united-states-masonic-founding-fathers/

the foundational streets and buildings in our cities. I do want to stress that even though many people have been deceived by the stated beliefs and practices of these secret organizations, God isn't at war with them and we shouldn't be either. Our war isn't with them, but with the spiritual forces of darkness that is holding them captive. Our Father wants them to understand truth, come out of that darkness and be saved. He doesn't want anyone to perish, but sometimes people's hearts and minds are so darkened by the deception of sin, they refuse to acknowledge the light of truth when it is presented. We need to pray people free from the darkness that blinds them to what path they're on.

We have explored the reasons why Satan has a detailed agenda to ruin God's ultimate plan, in hopes of delaying the kingdom of God from overtaking the earth. He knows he can't stop it entirely, but Satan works overtime to try to slow it down as much as possible. We delved into the topics of how occult symbols are tied to demonic power, and how the dominant power in any particular area is the ruler over those that reside there. We have also gone into some detail regarding how personal belief systems affect character. Character determines the results of personal choices, actions and behavior; the sum of these (especially collectively, in any given area) can either produce stability or instability: in people, families, organizations, communities, cities, political structures and governmental authority. Stability or instability lies in where people have anchored their trust. What is yours anchored to?

We see a great deal of instability in our world. All one needs to do is open their eyes. The emergence of more and more whistleblowers loudly proclaiming truth has exposed deeper levels of personal, corporate and political corruption like never before. People who spoke of conspiracy theories used to be considered paranoid, weird or accused of being influenced by a wrong spirit. With the age of the internet and massive exposure taking place, many of those so-called conspiracy theories are worth reconsideration. Things that were once considered too far-fetched to be taken seriously are suddenly found to be truth. The level of corruption and evil has been staggering. It takes time for people to accept this level of betrayal. The first reaction is unbelief. The second is shock, and anger. The third response is decision making, and the fourth is action. People must come to terms with what they can live with, and what they refuse to live with. The last level of response is when people come to a decision what they will do about the problem. They must reach a point of feeling compelled to take action, and decide what part they are personally willing to get involved in for the sake of change.

Governments and world powers collide with one another, fund both sides of wars and betray the people; while the elite (the puppet masters), pull the strings. The elite control the rest of the population. They own the banking system, the federal reserve, world systems, politicians, government officials and have a very long reach. Is there a way to turn the tables? **Absolutely.** God has already written the victory into the script! He just needs our cooperation to bring it to pass. Isn't it time to get on the winning team? Come on over to the Lord's side! If you read the Bible you'll discover that God is God, and Satan is a defeated foe. We continue to fight the good fight of faith. God always, always has a plan to outwit the proud, godless people that mock His authority. Our father knows how to overthrow evil plans, but it starts with prayer. It starts with you and I.

The reason all this is important is because we've been talking about ungodly foundations. The Masonic influence is in just about every city. Evil altars and thrones where iniquity and idolatry are practiced, empower Satan's rulership in our cities. It's always a battle for dominion. If Christians will not exercise the dominion God gave them, the devil will take the land. It's your possession and inheritance from God. Are you willing to fight for your land, your inheritance? Are you willing to exercise the dominion God gave you through the power of prayer? This is your city! This is our nation. It doesn't belong to the devil!

The mixture of beliefs perverts truth. Truth and error are not cohesive; they cannot form a strong foundation. The perverse spirit twists truth and promotes witchcraft and rebellion. Masonic Lodges are not the only thing that create thrones of iniquity. Abortion clinics, where innocent lives are sacrificed, become thrones of iniquity also. Many witches and Satanists work in abortion clinics. New Age establishments where false gods are worshipped, and witchcraft books and objects used in occult practices are sold, are another one. Kids that play with Ouija boards open up a demonic door. So do teens that play around with love spells they pick up in any number of clothing stores. Many of them sell them right there along with the fashion accessories. Seems innocent, but it's not. They don't know they are essentially building a throne to demonic spirits when they do that sort of thing, but it's true. Any place where people gather to seek spirits other than the Holy Spirit of Jesus Christ become altars and thrones where Satan is exalted. Homes where drugs, alcoholism, pornography, anger and other sins continually practiced can becomes thrones of evil. People don't understand that though. It's not just witches or those practicing sorcery that erect evil thrones. It's where ever rebellion, idolatry, and evil practices are exalted. It's where God is absent. When God's presence is absent, that void is filled with other things.

All of these contribute to laying evil foundations in a city. Evil altars are built in the unseen spiritual realm because forces of spiritual darkness found places where people came into agreement with them. They are strong, and they are there to protect their domain. These principalities and powers must be dismantled. Evil thrones and altars must be torn down and demonic entities evicted. These demonic principalities and powers are very strong forces that influence cities and geographical regions where they exist. They block prayer, oppress people, influence them to be angry, fearful, bitter, rebellious and many other things. Principalities and powers exercise their ability to influence others, much like a black ominous cloud.

"There were those who dwelt in darkness and in the shadow of death, prisoners in misery and chains, because they had rebelled against the words of God and spurned the counsel of the Most High..." Psalm 107:10,11.

When a people have turned away from God, He gives them time to repent. But, when a prolonged period of time has passed and the people's level of repentance is not sufficient to please God, sooner or later they can expect the occurrence of a certain progression of events. Drought comes across the land. Agriculture suffers. Provision begins to dry up and becomes increasingly more expensive.. Sickness and infirmity, depression, even mental illness increase. These are all effects of the curse against disobedience and idolatry. If the people still don't turn back to God, the protection over their borders is lifted and foreign enemies invade to threaten their existence. The threat of war becomes very real. Does any of this sound familiar? Look at where we are at today. ISIS has hundreds if not thousands of training camps within our country and multitudes of illegal aliens and refugees flood across our borders on a daily basis. All of this is happening, and there is one way to halt the advance of death and destruction: Repentance, and prayer.

We aren't going to overthrow evil dynasties, unseat wicked world rulers or outwit the enemy by thinking the world's justice system will prevail. It's sad, but true, and a great deal of what we see in the news today is proof that justice seems to be very flexible depending on who you are and who you know. Many of the world's corrupt elite have proven they are above the laws of the land. They are being protected by people who are helping to thwart justice. **The only way to accomplish change and overthrow evil is by doing it God's way, through humility and repentance.**

Isaiah 58 holds a key to opening the heavens. God instructed His people to stop mistreating one another and engaging in strife and debate; He told them to humble themselves and start treating others with kindness. When they did, their healing would spring forth quickly.

"No, this is the kind of fasting I want: Free those who are

wrongly imprisoned; lighten the burden of those who work for you. Let the oppressed go free, and remove the chains that bind people. Share your food with the hungry, and give shelter to the homeless. Give clothes to those who need them, and do not hide from relatives who need your help. "Then your salvation will come like the dawn, and your wounds will quickly heal. Your godliness will lead you forward, and the glory of the LORD will protect you from behind." Isaiah 58:6-8 NLT

Prayers of renouncement <u>are</u> important, but I don't want to sound like a broken record. **We must lean on the Lord and listen for strategy.** Various individuals will have a different piece of revelation and understanding, so we need to listen to one another. Hear what God is saying through others. One person might be passionate about prayer, another about public outreach, others for worship gatherings, and still others may understand the importance of mapping their city and going on prayer walks. They are all important and vital components working towards breakthrough. Each one is a strategy, and as a body we must come together to support one another in those important activities. God may also lead people to do some prophetic acts that may seem odd, but we often don't realize the power and effectiveness that come from acts of obedience. We've done all of these things. All the prophets of old conducted prophetic acts as a means of demonstrating a spiritual principle. When done in obedience to the leading of the

Holy Spirit, these things put fear in the heart of the enemy because they are anointed for breakthrough.[25] There are many wonderful things happening in the body of Christ in a variety of places. People are finding creative ways to touch their communities with the power and presence of God, and demonstrate His love to others. When we consider ways to effect cultural change, things such as prayer, prophetic declarations, worship, acts of kindness and mercy towards others are all powerful and effective means to impact others. They all work together as a means to help transform society.

---

[25] Ex. Refer to: Judges 7:13-25; Jer. 19:1-3; Ezek. 37:1-14

CHAPTER SIX

IDENTIFYING THE STRONGMAN

"Or else how can one enter a strong man's house and plunder his goods, unless he first binds the strong man? And then he will plunder his house" Matt. 12:29

A few years ago, I had been praying for my city, and I was hammering away in prayer pretty hard. One night I had a dream and I knew the interpretation of it. God showed me I was sitting in the strong man's house, and it involved a very powerful form of witchcraft known as Voodoo. I will go into more detail on that subject later, but I knew the Lord wanted to show me exactly how to pray in order to be more effective.

"When a strongman, fully armed, guards his own palace, his goods are in peace. But when a stronger than he comes upon him, he takes from him all his armor in which he trusted, and divides all his spoils. " *Luke 11:21,22 NKJV*

"For our struggle is not against flesh and blood enemies, but against evil rulers and authorities of the unseen world, against mighty powers in this dark world, and against evil spirits in the heavenly places. " Ephesians 6:12 NLT

A strongman is a ruler of darkness. Think of it like a general in an army. The general is the higher ranking demon, with other demons of lesser rank under his authority. Knowing how to defeat any army requires learning about their generals, military tactics, and how they operate. Military leaders also recognize the importance of knowing their enemy's weaknesses. So it is with spiritual strongmen. When you learn how to identify the manifestations of spiritual darkness, it becomes easier to then identify the strongman at work.

In scripture, a strongman is sometimes referenced as a person that has supernatural attributes. There are rulers in the earthly realm as well, that seem to receive supernatural assistance to carry out evil plots and destructive means. When people give themselves over to doing evil, evil comes to empower them, because Satan must find willing accomplices to carry out his plans for destruction. Cindy Jacobs, a respected apostolic Christian leader recognized for her ability to rally the troops to prayer, describes this as the law of double reference. Supernatural beings stand behind human structures, using them as a tool to carry out evil plans, such as Idi Amin, the former military dictator and President of Uganda; Adolph Hitler, the German dictator and founder of Nazism; and Joseph Stalin, former political power and Premier of the Soviet Union. Each of these powerful rulers were known for their horrendous crimes against humanity, including political repression, ethnic persecution and mass murders for the purposes of ethnic cleansing. There are difference names and faces today, but there are still individuals that are demonically empowered to carry out evil plans. Satan has people around them to act as evil shield bearers, protecting them from being brought to justice. Goliath of old had a shield bearer, too. We have heard many stories of David fighting Goliath, but I don't think I've ever heard it mentioned that David had to get past Goliath's shield bearer. [26]

This is a clue that offers us some additional wisdom. In able to remove a Goliath it is important to address the shield bearer(s) protecting the giant. Through prayer we can speak blindness into with the evil eyes that watch for ways to protect evildoers from the consequences of their actions. These are the people who are used to protect the person that represents the strongman. One way to target them in prayer is to ask God to send His weapons to target their blind spot. The enemy knows how to target people in their

---

[26] Ref. 1 Samuel 17:7

weakness; we must understand this strategy and repay the favor! Their blind spot is their vulnerable spot, their weakness that they do not realize anyone would stop to think about. God knows just where it is, and we need to pray into those areas. He can turn a heart or remove someone from position in a moment. When the shield bearers are removed, it is easier to take down the giants.

These ruling spirits are invisible entities in the heavenly realms. Cindy Jacobs, in her article *"Overcoming the Strongman"* writes, "One of the mightiest ways God displays His strength, however, is through a church that prevails through prayer. So, if Satan has been able to set up his thrones and dominion through wicked rulers, it's because the church has not been overpowering the strongman in intercession."[27]

Each strongman has lower ranking spirits assigned underneath them. If people are ignorant of the enemy's devices demons will team up against them and hold them in bondage. If people are not filled with the Holy Spirit, they are at a terrible disadvantage. Jesus told His disciples in Acts chapter one to wait for the promise of the Holy Spirit before they went out to evangelize. He knew they

---

[27] Jacobs: *"Overcoming the Strongman"*, August 17, 2015, Generals International; https://www.generals.org/articles/single/overcoming-the-strongman/

needed the power to effectively combat things they would encounter. Far too many times people waste their time trying to resolve problems in their own strength or with their own reason. Demonic spirits just mock God's people and do what they please – unless, and until – the people of God start demonstrating the power of God is with them to heal the sick, cast out demons, raise the dead and witness to the power of God's kingdom. ***We cannot heal, deliver or witness to God's power without the infilling of the Holy Spirit.*** He has the gifts and the power! The first thing people need in order to be successful in effecting their cities with cultural change is the baptism of the Holy Spirit. [28]When people begin to be successful in their battle against the demonic spirits that seek to oppress them, then they can begin to advance the kingdom of God. If there is little to no advancement of the kingdom of God, then we know that it is because so few people are truly walking in their true identity as victorious sons and daughters of God.

The following is a list of spiritual strongmen as well as the fruit of how those spirits manifest in a person's life. Spirits team up with one another under the strongman. This will help you understand some of the ways they link up together. Many of these examples were taken from Drs. Jerry (Gerald) and Carol Robeson's book, *"Strongman's His Name…What's His Game?"*

---

[28] Ref. Acts 1:8; 2:2:1-4; 2:12; 2:14-21.

(Robeson: Whitaker House, © 1984) I also included some additional references of my own.

Strongman	Characteristics / Manifestations	Scripture References	Comments
Spirit of Divination	Fortune teller, soothsayer, warlock, satanist, Witch/Wiccan, Druid-Pagan, Astrology and Horoscopes, Rebellion, Hypnotist, Enchanter, Drugs (Greek. - Pharmakos), Waterwitching/ Divination, Magic Divination	Acts 16:16-18; Micah 5:12; Isaiah 2:6; Exodus 22:18; Isaiah 47:13; Leviticus 19:26; Jeremiah 10:2; 1 Samuel 15:23; Deuteronomy 18:11; Isaiah 19:3; Galatians 5:20;	**Bind:** the Spirit of Divination **Loose:** The Holy Spirit and Gifts, 1 Corinthians 12:7-12 (My additions: **Bind:** Spirit of Leviathan, Bitterness, Pride **Loose:** Humility, a Spirit of Repentance,

	...(continued)	Revelation 9:21; 18:23; 21:8; 22:15; Hosea 4:12; Exodus 7:11; 8:7; 9:11	the Love of God, God's grace)
Familiar Spirit	Necromancer, Medium, Peeping and Muttering, Yoga, Clairvoyant, Spiritist, Drugs (Greek. - Pharmakos), Passive Mind Dreamers, False Prophecy (My additions: voyeurism, Kundalini spirit)	Deuteronomy 18:11; 1 Chronicles 10:13; 1 Samuel 28; Isaiah 8:19; 29:4; 59:3; Jeremiah 29:8; 1 Samuel 28:7,8; Galatians 5:20; Revelations 9:21; 18:23; 21:8; 22:15	**Bind**: Familiar Spirits **Loose**: Holy Spirit and Gifts, 1 Corinthians 12:9-12

Spirit of Jealousy	Murder Revenge-Spite, Anger-Rage, Jealousy, Hatred, Cruelty, Strife, Contention, Competition, Envy, Cause Divisions	Scriptures: (Genesis 4:4-6; 37:3,4,8; Proverbs 6:34; 10:12; 13:10; 14:16-17,29-30; 22:24-25; 27:4; 29:22-23; Numbers 5:14,30; 1 Thessalonians 4:8; Song of Solomon 8:6; Galatians 5:19)	**Bind:** Spirit of jealousy **Loose:** Love of God, 1 Corinthians 13; Ephesians 5:2
Lying Spirit	Strong Deceptions, Flattery, Superstitions, Religious Bondages, False Prophecy,	2 Chron. 18:22; Psalms 31:18; 78:36; Proverbs 6:16- 19; 10:18; 20:19;	**Bind:** Lying Spirit **Loose:** Spirit of Truth, (Father God, Jesus, Holy Spirit and The

	Accusations, Slander, Gossip, Lies, False Teachers	26:28; 29:5; Jeremiah 23:16-17; 27:9,10; Matthew 7:15; 2 Thes. 2:9-13; 1 Timothy 4:7; 6:20; 2 Tim. 2:16; 2 Peter; 1 John 3-5; Revelation 12:10	Word of God) John 4:23-24; 8:32, 14:17; 15:26; 16:13; 17:17; 1 John 3:24-4:6
Perverse Spirit.	Broken Spirit, Evil Actions, Atheist, Abortion, Child Abuse, Filthy Mind, Doctrinal Error, Sex Perversions, Twisting The Word, Foolish, Chronic	Exodus 20:13; 21:22-25; Proverbs 1:22; 2:12; 14:2; 15:4; 17:20,23; 19:1,3; 23:33; Isaiah 19:14; Acts 13:10; Romans	**Bind:** Perverse Spirit, (My additions) Spirit of Chemosh **Loose:** God's Spirit; Purity, Holiness, Zechariah 12:10; Hebrews

	Worrier, Contentions, Incest, Pornography, (My additions: Lust, masturbation, incubus/succubus spirits, sexual addiction)	1:17-32; Philippians 2:14-16; 1 Timothy 6:4,5; 2 Timothy 3:2,7-8; Titus 3:11,11; 2 Peter 2:14	10:29; 12:14 (My addition: spirit of humility and repentance, liberty) Break the power of Chemosh (see 1 Kings 11:7,33) and any curses of bloodline curses from incest also.
Spirit of Haughtiness	Arrogant-Smug, Pride, Idleness, Scornful, Strife, Obstinate, Self-Deception, Contentious, Self-Righteous, Rebellion, Rejection of	1 Samuel 15:23; 2 Samuel 22:8; Proverbs 1:22; 3:34; 6:16,17; 10:4; 13:10; 16:18,19;	**Bind:** Spirit of Haughtiness **Loose:** Humble and Contrite Spirit, Proverbs 16:19; Romans

	God	21:24; 24:9; 28:25; 29:1,8; Jeremiah 43:2; 48:29; 49:16; Isaiah 2:11,17; 5:15; 16:6; Ezekiel 16:49-50; Daniel 5:20; Obadiah 1:3; Luke 18:11,12	1:4
Spirit of Heaviness	Excessive Mourning, Sorrow-Grief, Insomnia, Self-Pity, Rejection, Broken-Heart, Despair, Dejection, Hopelessness, Depression,	Isaiah 61:3; Luke 4:18; Nehemiah 2:2; Proverbs 15:13; Psalms 69:20; Proverbs 12:18; 15:3,13;	**Bind:** Spirit of Heaviness **Loose:** Comforter, Garment of Praise, Oil of Joy, John 15:26; Isaiah 61:3

		Suicide, Inner Hurts, Torn Spirit, Heaviness	18:14; Luke 4:18; 2 Corinthians 1:8-9; Isaiah 61:3; Mark 9; Luke 4:18; Proverbs 18:14; 26:22	
Spirit of Whoredom		Unfaithfulness, Adultery, Spirit-Soul-or-Body Prostitution, Chronic Dissatisfaction, Love of Money, Fornication, Idolatry, Excessive Appetite, Worldliness	Ezekiel 16:15,28; Proverbs 5:1-14; Galatians 5:19; Deuteronomy 23:17-18; Ezekiel 16:28; Proverbs 15:27; 1 Timothy 6:7-14; Hosea 4:13-19; Judges 2:17; Ezekiel 16;	**Bind:** Spirit of Whoredom **Loose:** Spirit of God: Pure Spirit, Holiness, Commitment, Insatiable Ever Increasing Hunger for more of God Spirit and Presence, Ephesians 3:16; John 3:34; 14:12

		Leviticus 17:7; 1 Corinthians 6:13-16; Philippians 3:19; James 4:4	
Spirit of Infirmity	Bent Body-Spine, Impotent, Frail, Lame, Asthma-Hay Fever-Allergies, Arthritis, Weakness, Lingering Disorders, Oppression, Cancer, (My additions: lingering unexplained illness and disease; breakdown of	Luke 13:11; John 5:5; Acts 3:2; 4:9; Acts 10:38	**Bind:** Spirit of Infirmity **Loose:** Spirit of life and gifts of healing, Romans 8:2; 1 Corinthians 12:9

		the body).		
Deaf and Dumb Spirit	Dumb-Mute, Crying, Drown, Tearing, Blindness, Mental Illness, Ear Problems, Suicidal, Foaming At The Mouth, Seizures/ Epilepsy, Burn, Gnashing Of Teeth, Pining Away, Prostration	Matt. 9:32,33; 12:22; 15:30-31; 17:15; Mark 5:5; 9:18,22,25-26,39 Luke 9:39	**Bind:** Deaf and Dumb Spirit **Loose:** Resurrection Life and Gifts OF Healing, Romans 8:11; 1 Corinthians 12:9
Spirit of Bondage	Fears, Addictions (Drugs, Alcohol, Cigarettes, Food,	Rom. 6:16; 7:23; 8:15; 2 Peter 2:19; Heb. 2:14-15; Luke 8:23; John	**Bind:** Spirit of Bondage **Loose:** Liberty, Spirit of Adoption, Romans 8:15

	Masturbation and sexual sins) Fear of Death, Captivity to Satan, Servant of Corruption, Compulsive Sin, Bondage to Sin	8:34; Acts 8:23; Proverbs 5:2; 2 Tim. 2:26	
Spirit of Fear	Fears, Phobias, Heart Attacks, Torment-Horror, Fear of Man, Nightmares, Terrors, Anxiety-Stress, Fear of Death, Untrusting, Doubt	Isaiah 13:7-8; 2 Tim. 1:7; Psalms 55:4-5; 1 John 4:18; Luke 21:26; John 14:1,27; Prov. 29:25; Jer. 1:8; 17-19; Ezek. 2:6-7; 3:9; Psalms 91:5-6; Isaiah 54:14; Heb.	**Bind:** Spirit of Fear **Loose:** Love, Power, and A Sound Mind; Perfect Love casts out all fear, 2 Timothy 1:7; 1 John 4:18

		2:14-15; 1 Peter 5:7; Matt.8:26; Rev. 21:8	
Seducing Spirits	Hypocritical Lies, Seared Conscience, Attractions, Fascinations by false prophets, signs and wonders, Deception, Wandering from the Truth, Fascination with evil ways objects or persons, Seducers, Enticers	1 Tim.4:1; Proverbs 12:22; James 1:14; Mark 13:22; Rom. 7:11; 2 Thes. 2:10; 2 Tim. 3:13; 1 John 2:18-26; Deut. 13:6-8; 2 Tim. 3:13; Prov. 1:10; 12:26; 2 Tim. 3:13	**Bind:** Seducing Spirits **Loose:** Holy Spirit - Truth, John 16:13
Spirit of Anti-Christ	Denies Deity of Christ, Denies Atonement,	1 John 2:18,19; 4:3,5; 2 John	**Bind:** Spirit of Anti-Christ **Loose:** Spirit

	Against Christ and His Teaching, Humanism, Worldly Speech and Actions, Teachers of Heresies, Anti-Christian, Deceiver, Lawlessness	1:7; 2 Thes. 2:4, 3-12; Rev. 13:7	of Truth, 1 John 4:6
Spirit of Abandonment	Isolation Victim Mentality Rejection, Loneliness Feels unwanted, Feels unloved,	Ps. 27:10-14; Heb. 13:5; Eph. 1:6	**Bind:** Spirit of Abandonment **Loose:** Spirit of Adoption, Rom. 5:8
Leviathan/ Pride (My addition)	Stubborn, Lying, Hardheaded, Stubborn, Debating, Insubordinate,	Job 41:34	**Bind:** Spirit of Leviathan and Pride **Loose:** Humility, Grace of God,

	Argumentative, Mocking, Scoffer		Spirit of Repentance
Spirit of Insanity/Mental Illness (My addition)	Obsessive-compulsive Confusion, Compulsions, Insanity, Schizophrenia, Paranoia, Hallucinations, Hysteria	Deut. 28:20-28, 2 Tim. 1:7	**Bind:** Spirit of Insanity/Mental Illness **Loose:** Power of God, Love and a sound mind, 2 Tim. 1:7
Spirit of Death	Unexplained terminal health issues, untimely death, extreme poverty	Prov. 18:21, Eph. 4:18, 1 John 5:12, Rev. 6:5,6, Deut. 28:20-28, Rom 6:16, Rom. 8:13,	**Bind:** Spirit of Death and Hell Loose: Holy spirit/Spirit of Resurrection life, Gifts of Holy Spirit, Rom. 8:2
Spirit of Apollyon/ Abaddon (My addition)	Destruction, car accidents, self-defeating behaviors,	Rev. 9:11, Exodus 10:12-20; Joel 1:4, 2:4-	**Bind:** Spirit of Apollyon/ Abaddon **Loose:** Spirit

	torment, near death experiences, financial destruction, things that devour	14, Ezekiel 2:6, Lk 11:12	of Repentance, humility

When we attack an enemy, we must chase it all the way back to where it came from. Jesus gave us the example. When He was crucified and died upon the cross, He was only there for a short time. Where do you think he went for three days? They put Him in the tomb but death couldn't hold him, so He went to the lowermost parts of the earth and returned with the keys of death and hell. Do you understand? He didn't call. He didn't text. He didn't send a Facebook message. The Spirit of Death couldn't hold Him. He got up from where he was and deliberately did something to take back what belonged to Him. What is it *you* need to do? Jesus went straight into the house of the enemy, took the keys of the house and spoiled every plan of the enemy. When we battle against an enemy, we need to follow that enemy all the way back to the house. Devils will run for home but we have to possess their gates and recover the spoils. In order to do that, you've got to be willing to walk into the devil's house and demand he give back everything he took.

The assignments of the enemy against the children of God are widely varied and often tailored to suit the individual. I do not suggest that everything a person encounters is the result of a demon; however, the reality is, there are a lot of instances where people tend to ignore the possibility that demonic influences are at work to create the problems and difficulties that occur in their daily lives. We can't solve natural problems if we ignore the fact that many are spiritually rooted. Many of the above listed characteristics are not merely 'symptoms and behaviors,' but actual demonic spirits by the same name.

Some of these spirits can be recognized by their symptoms and cast out, while others cannot. Some areas of deliverance can only come by the additional component of fasting. We each need to cooperate with God in working towards self-deliverance and inner healing. And, while there will be times when it becomes necessary to seek out anointed people to pray for us, that alone cannot be seen as a substitute for taking responsibility for our sin issues. Our Father wants us to learn and experience is the best teacher. Once a person has been delivered from something, they better understand how to identify it in others and lead them towards their freedom. It is for our own benefit to cooperate with God and His Holy Spirit so that we may achieve greater levels of inner healing and freedom. The more freedom we gain, the greater ability we have to possess our promises and take hold of our spiritual inheritance.

It is an unfortunate fact that many people, including Christian leaders, resist practicing deliverance simply because of a lack of knowledge, or a belief system that is based in spiritual error. While Jesus did come to break the curse we were under, we still have to fight for it. We still need to exercise the dominion God gave us. Any teaching that says that we don't need to do these things is based in error. Some people feel awkward with the idea of spiritual warfare. They have adopted the mindset that tells them Jesus did it all and therefore they have no need to fight the devil. Others may suggest that 'we don't give the devil any attention; we focus on Jesus.' I once belonged to a church that downplayed the spiritual warfare aspect, but this too is based on error. That is not what the Bible teaches.

Scripture reminds us:

- Not to give place to the devil, Eph. 4;27
- Beware of the devil that seeks to devour, 1 Peter 5:8,9
- Avoid the snare of the devil, 1 Tim. 3:7
- Use our weapons to pull down strongholds, 2 Cor. 10:4

- We fight spiritual wickedness in high places, Eph. 6:12
- Resist the devil and make him flee, James 4:6,7
- We do not fight in our own strength but by God's spirit, Zech. 4:6
- We are to put on the armor of God, preparing us for battle; Eph. 6:13
- Be strong and courageous against the enemies we fight; Joshua 10:25

Spiritual warfare, like anything else, is learned. If a person is not used to praying against the schemes of the enemy, they may feel intimidated or insecure about praying that way. The devil isn't threatened by wishy-washy prayers. He knows when people understand their authority in Christ. That doesn't mean a person needs to go around yelling at the devil all the time, but it does indicate a need to be confident of your identity in Christ.

God is heartbroken over the fact that His people are destroyed over a lack of knowledge. Why were they destroyed? Because they rejected knowledge.

"Therefore My people go into exile for their lack of knowledge; And their honorable men are famished, And their multitude is parched with thirst." Isaiah 5:13

"My people are being destroyed because they don't know me. Since you priests refuse to know me, I refuse to recognize you as my priests. Since you have forgotten the laws of your God, I will forget to bless your children." Hosea 4:6

When people lack knowledge or understanding in a particular area they may tend to become defensive in order to redirect the attention away from the topic that makes them feel awkward, uncomfortable and vulnerable.

The reality is, spiritually rooted issues will not go away just because we refuse to talk about it. Familiar spirits that attach themselves to different family lines are assigned to us long before we have any awareness of it. Many people are born into spiritual bondage that they have no way of knowing exists. I was 47 years old before the Lord revealed in a dream two very strong demonic spirits that were assigned to me from before my birth. This is how Satan perpetuates cycles of brokenness, spiritual bondage, and manifests the effects of a curse into the future generations.

Every person needs the benefit of the word of God, and deliverance and healing are very much in the word of God. We were created to prosper from personal relationship with the word of God, because the word is synonymous with Jesus.

"In the beginning was the Word, and the Word was with God, and the Word was God." John 1:1 NIV

"The Word became flesh and made his dwelling among us. We have seen his glory, the glory of the one and only Son, who came from the Father, full of grace and truth." John 1:14 NIV

The word of God is likened to bread that feeds our souls. Various times in scripture Jesus refers to Himself as the Bread of Life. The word of God is also compared to food that contains supernatural power and ability nourish, heal and deliver us.

Jesus said to them, "I am the bread of life; whoever comes to me shall not hunger, and whoever believes in me shall never thirst." ESV

"For the word of God is living and active, sharper than any two-edged sword, piercing to the division of soul and of spirit, of joints and of marrow, and discerning the thoughts and intentions of the heart." Hebrews 4:12 ESV

"The Spirit gives life; the flesh counts for nothing. The words I have spoken to you--they are full of the Spirit and life." John 6:63 NIV

"He sent out his word and healed them, and delivered them from their destruction." Psalm 107:20 ESV

Binding and loosing are actions that either 'tie up and secure' or 'untie and release.' I love the way the Aramaic Bible in Plain English writes the scripture in Matthew 16:19.

"To you I shall give the keys of the Kingdom of Heaven; everything that you will bind in the earth will have been bound in Heaven, and anything that you will release in the earth will have been released in Heaven."

Did you notice that it reflects *'past'* tense? What we bind on earth has already been bound in heaven; what we loose on earth has already been released in heaven. *It's already been done.* As ambassadors from a royal kingdom, all we have to do is enforce the laws of our homeland! Friend, you've been given the authority to either permit or deny certain things through prayer. Jesus gave us authority to bind and loose in Matthew 18:18. That means we can either excommunicate demons - and send them packing - or we can allow their evil deeds to continue. When we exercise the authority God gave us, we can liberate people from the chains of oppression. We can untie them from demonic attachments of sin. We get to partake of the blessing along with Christ in breaking off guilt, shame, rejection, condemnation and deliver people from the curses that plague them. There is so much joy in the work of the Lord! Even in the midst of trials it becomes easier to understand how of Jesus it was said, *"...who for the joy that was set before Him endured the cross..." Hebrews 12:2*

Identifying the Strongman

As I was praying over my city a few years ago, the Lord gave me a dream that I was sitting in the strongman's house. I had never stopped to think about that before, but God showed me that there was a very strong spirit of voodoo over my city. He drew a connection between where I lived and New Orleans, and I knew He was communicating that the spiritual strongman was in fact the same sort of occult magic that is prevalent in New Orleans.

I found that a bit startling, because Escondido and New Orleans are two very different cities, in very different places on the map. The culture of these two cities appears vastly different. However, as I continue to pray, I started to see some of the ways they shared some similarities. Then I realized that these same dynamics go far beyond just Escondido and New Orleans. The spiritually rooted issues can affect many cities in this nation.

A Wikipedia article on New Orleans Voodoo has this to say:

"Voodoo was brought to French Louisiana during the colonial period by workers and slaves from West Africa. From 1719 to 1731, the majority of African captives brought as slaves to Louisiana were Fon people from what is now Benin; other groups such as the Bambara, Mandinga, Wolof, Ewe, Fulbe, Nard, Mina, Fon (Dahomean),Yoruba (Nago), Chamba, Congo, Ibo, Ado, Hausa, and Sango (Hall) also brought their cultural practices, languages, and religious beliefs rooted in spirit and ancestor worship. All of the groups were responsible for the development of Louisiana Voodoo. Their knowledge of herbs, poisons, and the ritual creation of charms and amulets, intended to protect oneself or harm others, became key elements of Louisiana Voodoo. [29] Louisiana voodoo has existed since the early 1700s."[30]

"Newly arrived Africans dominated the slave community. According to a census of 1731-1732, the ratio of enslaved Africans to European settlers was more than two to one. As a relatively small number of colonists were planters and slaveholders, the Africans were held in large groups, which enabled their preservation of African practices and culture." Unlike in the Upper

---

[29] Hall, Gwendolyn Midlo (1995). Africans in Colonial Louisiana: The Development of Afro-Creole Culture in the Eighteenth Century. Louisiana State University Press. p. 58.

[30] *New Orleans Voodoo*, Wikipedia, the Free Encyclopedia, https://en.wikipedia.org/wiki/Louisiana_Voodoo

South, where different groups were brought together and slave families were frequently divided among different plantations, in southern Louisiana families, cultures and languages were kept more intact." [31]

"Under the French code and the influence of Catholicism, officials nominally recognized family groups, prohibiting the sale of slave children away from their families if younger than age fourteen."[32] "The high mortality of the slave trade brought its survivors together with a sense of solidarity and initiation. The absence of fragmentation in the enslaved community, along with the kinship system produced by the bond created by the difficulties of slavery, resulted in a "coherent, functional, well integrated, autonomous, and self-confident enslaved community."[33]

The practice of making and wearing charms and amulets for protection, healing, or the harm of others was a key aspect to early Louisiana Voodoo. [34] "The Ouanga, a charm used to poison an enemy, contained the toxic roots of the *figuier maudit tree*, brought

---

[31] Hall (1995). Africans in Colonial Louisiana. pgs. 159-162.

[32] Hall (1995). Africans in Colonial Louisiana. p. 168.

[33] Hall (1995). Africans in Colonial Louisiana. p. 159.

[34] Hall (1995). Africans in Colonial Louisiana. p. 163.

from Africa and preserved in Louisiana. The ground-up root was combined with other elements, such as bones, nails, roots, holy water, holy candles, holy incense, holy bread, or crucifixes. The administrator of the ritual frequently evoked protection from Jehovah and Jesus Christ. This openness of African belief allowed for the adoption of Catholic practices into Louisiana Voodoo." [35]

"As a result of the fusion of Francophone culture and Voodoo in Louisiana, Creole African Americans associated many Voodoo spirits with the Christian saints known to preside over the same domain. Although some doctrinaire leaders of each tradition believe Voodoo and Catholic practices are in conflict, in popular culture both saints and spirits are believed to act as mediators, with the Catholic priest or voodoo Legba presiding over specific respective activities. Early followers of Voodoo in the United States adopted the image of the Catholic saints to represent their spirits." [36] "Other Catholic practices adopted into Louisiana Voodoo include reciting the Hail Mary and the Lord's Prayer." [37]

---

[35] Hall (1995). Africans in Colonial Louisiana. p. 165.

[36] Jacobs, Claude F. & Andrew J. Kaslow (2001). The Spiritual Churches of New Orleans: Origins, Beliefs, and Rituals of an African-American Religion. University of Tennessee Press.

[37] Nickell, Joe (2006). "Voodoo in New Orleans". The Skeptical Inquirer.

Santeria and Lucumi are also forms of witchcraft practices that merge the spiritual practices of people from Cuba, Puerto Rico, the Dominican Republic (who were also Roman Catholics) and tribes from West Africa. Slaves who were brought to America were forced to convert religions, but in order to hold on to some of their own religious traditions and customs, including divination or calling to spirits of the dead, animal sacrifice, sacred drumming and dance, they incorporated their native West African traditions into the Catholic icons and renamed them. They still referred to them as saints. It became a mixture of witchcraft practices. The perverse spirit connected to witchcraft produces spiritual error and carries a curse. Santeria is influenced by and syncretized with Roman Catholicism. Its liturgical language, a dialect of Yoruba, is also known as Lucumí.[38] Santeria and Lucumi have many rituals and ceremonies that are held in a house temple, or what is called a 'house of Saints.' The meetings are conducted by Priests or Priestesses. There is a display of 'thrones' that represents the kings, queens and deified warriors who are invoked for guidance and blessing. The 'disciples' of Santeria are given prayer beads as a sacred point of contact with the spirits called upon in these witchcraft ceremonies. After many rituals are performed, the

---

[38] "Santería". Religions of the World. Retrieved January 4, 2009.

^ "Lucumí Religion". New Orleans Mistic. Archived from the original on May 29, 2008. Retrieved January 4, 2009.

person is 'born again' into the faith. Not the Christian faith, but of the occult.

There is also a very strong link between Santeria, Lucemi and demonic sexual spirits such as incubus, succubus and lust. Some people suffer from demonic oppression from sexual spirits. If a person struggles with that type of oppression, there is a good chance that there is a demonic connection to some form of the occult. Spirits of Lust, Witchcraft, Mind Control, Perversion, Hatred and Immorality are interconnected by a demonic network through the sins of idolatry and rebellion. Even good, well meaning, church-going people can be guilty of idolatry and rebellion towards God if they do not understand the spiritual dynamics associated with their personal history. Please understand I am not passing judgment on anyone. I had a great deal in my own family history that I needed to deal with, so I understand that sometimes these things can come as a shock. Personal history also includes the religious roots of your family. A curse comes in when a door has been opened to the enemy. It affects the entire family for generations to come unless someone intentionally breaks those ungodly ties through prayers of renouncement. Only the blood of Jesus is powerful enough to break demonic attachments and the power of the curse.

There are many sincere, God loving Christians in the Catholic church and in a variety of churches. It's not my intent to be critical but to open people's eyes to certain religious practices and traditions that they may not understand can be quite harmful spiritually. When sin is not addressed, people suffer needlessly, the enemy gains power and the church loses its authority and power. The enemy takes advantage of our lack of knowledge and then it gives him opportunity to destroy, kill, and rob from people.

Martin Luther led the way into the reformation of the Catholic Church in the mid 1500's but there is still a great deal of truth yet to be restored to many churches, including the Catholic Church. When truth is restored, people are set free from the opposing spiritual forces that either put them in bondage or place constrictions on their faith. It is my hope to restore truth so that people can break free from ungodly systems and structures, get free from the difficulties that plague their lives and truly fulfill all that God has for them.

There are many things that people can do unknowingly that end up testing God or opening doors to the enemy simply out of ignorance to the ways spiritual principles operate. Just because one has been taught something from their youth, or relied on the teachings of others they trusted to tell them the truth, doesn't necessarily mean that what has been accepted is *actually* the truth. It is so important to read the Bible for ourselves so that we allow

God's Holy Spirit to teach us. It's His job to lead us into truth. Sometimes people aren't aware of spiritual ramifications to the things they do and they see nothing wrong with certain practices until someone helps them see the truth. These are things that have been introduced by man at some point in history and 'added to' the Word of God as though it came from God, or truth has been twisted to suit the personal viewpoint and convictions of various individuals. Then it is taught as though it's scriptural. We are never to alter the scriptures or twist them to suit our purposes. This is an effect of a perverse spirit. It also makes everything else unclean, no matter how many rituals are performed. It is an abomination to God and the persons affected may never realize that an unbroken curse exists.

"I testify to anyone that adds to the prophecy in this book: if anyone adds to them, God will add to them the plagues that are written in this book; and if anyone takes away from the words of the book of this prophecy, God will take away his part from the tree of life and from the holy city, which are written in this book..." Rev. 22:18,19

"Do not add to His words, or He will rebuke you and prove you a liar." Prov. 30:8

Many years ago, when I was very young, a woman I worked

with introduced me to prayer candles. I found out later she was a practicing witch. I was so naïve. I had no idea that they were used as a point of contact to invoke demonic spirits. At the time I was driven by desperation and completely unaware of how my actions affected me spiritually. It's a form of witchcraft and idolatry to call out in prayer to anyone, or any spirit, other than Jesus Christ, our Heavenly Father or Holy Spirit. The Bible never instructs us to pray to Mary or other saints because it is written in John 10:9,

"I am the gate; whoever enters through me will be saved. They will come in and go out, and find pasture."

Jesus alone is the door to the Father, to salvation, and to answered prayer. It is also written in Acts 4:12,

"Salvation is found in no one else, for there is no other name under heaven given to mankind by which we must be saved."

Therefore, praying to any other name, person, spirit or saint is a form of conjuring occult spirits to try to obtain wisdom, protection or get a need or desire answered through illegitimate means. What may seem innocent is not. It's an open invitation for devils to rob, steal and plunder. Calling on ANY OTHER spirit for help is idolatrous and summons demonic spirits, giving them permission to intervene in a person's life. Nowhere in the Bible does it ever say to pray to the virgin Mary, other saints, or call out to other names for assistance. Some people, especially those in the Catholic church, may stand upon the verse in Revelation 5:8-14 as a means of justifying praying to Mary or others that have passed on and are now in heaven. The problem is, **nowhere** in scripture does it say that praying to those in heaven is permitted, and nowhere in scripture does it indicate that they are to receive our prayers.

Jesus instructed His disciples to pray in Matthew 6:9 to pray to "Our Father." Jesus also instructed on the matter of whose name to ask when petitioning the Heavenly Father. HIS.

He said in John 14:13,14: *"And whatever you ask in My name, that I will do, that My Father will be glorified in the Son. If you ask anything in My name I will do it."*

Again in John 16:23 Jesus said, *"In that day you will no longer ask Me anything. Very truly I tell you, My Father will give you whatever you ask in My name."*

Here again we clearly see the intent of scripture is to direct our prayers to our Heavenly Father, asking in the name of Jesus. As a further matter of dispelling the doctrinal error of praying to Mary or other 'saints,' we can see the intent of scripture is also carried out in Acts 10:25,26. Cornelius threw himself at the Apostle

Peter's feet in a display of worship. "But Peter raised him up saying, *'Stand up; I too am just a man.'*"

The same thought is repeated in Acts 14:15 with Paul and Barnabus. The people of the city thought they were gods and began to worship them.

"But when the apostles Barnabas and Paul heard of it, they tore their robes and rushed out into the crowd, crying out and saying, "Men, why are you doing these things? We are also men of the same nature as you, and preach the gospel to you that you should turn from these vain things to a living God, WHO MADE THE HEAVEN AND THE EARTH AND THE SEA AND ALL THAT IS IN THEM."

In Revelation 19:10, the Apostle John had an encounter with an angel and wanted to honor the angel by bowing to him. *"At this I fell at his feet to worship him. But he said to me, "Don't do that! I am a fellow servant with you and with your brothers and sisters who hold to the testimony of Jesus. Worship God! For it is the Spirit of prophecy who bears testimony to Jesus."* As you can see, the intent of scripture is very clear. We do not seek angels, pray to them or petition anyone except God. Nowhere in scripture are we told that those in heaven can even hear the prayers from those on earth, or if they are allowed to. They are human, just like us, and they are probably very much involved in worshiping Jesus in heaven, but we have no way of knowing if they are granted prayer assignments or any such thing. There is just not enough documentation in scripture to try to justify this erroneous belief. Praying to the spirits of those that have passed on - even if they are in heaven - is seeking to obtain answers or help by going through someone other than Jesus, the Father, and Holy Spirit. Scripture is clear that those that practice such things are in rebellion and practicing idolatry. Idolatrous practices mean that people have broken covenant with their God, and because of this they suffer from effects of disobedience.

Luke 24:1-8 asks a powerful question. *"Why do you look for the living among the dead? He is not here!"* The dead, even the dead who are now in heaven, have no ability or power granted to them to answer prayer. Only God answers prayer. There are many other scriptures that state that only JESUS CHRIST has been given the power of salvation and deliverance to those who call on His name. No one else has that right to be called upon for help because no one else suffered for our sin or gave their life in our place. There are other practices, too, that are accepted in the Catholic religion but not biblical and actually go against scripture, such as turning to a priest to absolve a person's sins. While James chapter 5 does encourage us to adopt the practice of humility and confessing our sins that we might be healed, it does not mean that a human being is permitted to absolve sin. Priests have no power to cleanse a person from sin. Only God can atone for sin, and it only comes through the shed blood of Jesus. No amount of saying ritualistic prayers or good works can impute righteousness. ONLY the blood of Jesus takes away our sin. Only His blood imputes righteousness. Financial donations to the church, volunteering, good works - nothing else atones for sin. So, if a religion practices or promotes anything that trusts in anything outside of the Cross, Jesus blood or the prayer of faith to the Lord, then they are putting their trust and efforts in dead works.

The things people are 'in agreement with' has every bit to do with whether or not they are in agreement with God and submitted to Him, or in agreement with other spirits that are active in their life. The spirit realm sees it as being in a covenant partnership. The question each person should ask themselves is whether or not they are faithful to being in covenant with God, or if they have unknowingly made a covenant with some not-so-friendly 'other' spirits that have opened themselves up to a curse.

People, good people, desperate for a breakthrough, often do things they shouldn't. Like buying prayer candles and praying to various other spirits, powers, and saints. Good people can get so desperate that they will try just about anything to try to find relief from their situation. I know, because I used to do it too, but it's called witchcraft, idolatry, and rebellion towards God.

Many years ago our family was suffering from extreme hardship. All our work dried up. Phones broke. We couldn't even get a phone call to get work if someone *had* called us on a job. It literally felt like some unseen spiritual force was squeezing us to death. At the same time, I began having some very alarming dreams about witches and Satanists chasing us, trying to kill us. I knew God was trying to communicate something but I had no idea what it was. One night I prayed fervently for answers. After about half an hour of praying in the Spirit, I heard God say, "Renounce Voodoo." Ummm...*what???* My mind was suddenly arrested right where I was. I was shocked. I hesitated, then said, "I don't understand how that could be applicable, Lord." My head raced to try to make sense of what I heard, but I had a very strong feeling that He was waiting for me to be obedient to what He said. It literally felt like the Lord was standing right next to me. After a few moments, I started to pray again. This time, I began with confession and repentance, asking the Lord to forgive the sins associated with Voodoo and the occult. I felt like I was stumbling through it, but I included the sins of my ancestors, asking for the blood of Jesus to cover any doors that may have been opened by anyone in my family, myself included. When I had finished praying, I heard Him ask me, "Do you know what those in your family have opened a door to, Laura?" I said, "No, Lord...how could I possibly know that?" To which He responded, "That is my point exactly." What I really wanted to ask Him is why He waited so long to tell me. It's not like I had just gotten saved. That information could have been helpful a lot sooner! God has His timing though, and it taught me something else important to understand. Things can lie dormant in the spirit realm for a long time before Satan decides to act on them. We just never know what might be out there waiting to take us down. It pays to ask the Lord for the details! There can be many things that the spirit realm is quite aware of, but we are not, and it's those things that keep us blind to the doors the enemy uses to gain access to our lives.

That first step of renouncing Voodoo and witchcraft opened a door to a great deal more revelation. I began to remember memories that had been repressed, and in an instant Holy Spirit connected the dots, showing me how certain things were tied into occult spirits. Witchcraft and rebellion had been very strong in my family but I never realized that until the Lord revealed it. It was both a bit unsettling and fascinating to receive this sort of understanding. Many people are curious about their ancestry and the roots of where they came from because they feel it gives them a better sense of who they are. We should be just as interested in our spiritual ancestry too, because it also reveals a lot about why certain things are in our family history. Things like mental illness, depression, untimely deaths, recurring divorces, incest, molestation and many other things can all be spiritually rooted in generational sin patterns.

Permit me, if you will, to bounce back to something that was stated earlier. I'm going to connect some more dots. Many years ago, during the time when black slaves were being imported to America, they were brought from Africa and Caribbean islands. African Muslims were imported along with the slaves. "African religious beliefs, including knowledge of herbs, poisons and the creation of charms and amulets of support or power, came to Louisiana with the earliest contingents of slaves. All adult Bumbara males knew how to make charms. There are examples of slaves being accused of being poisoners during the 1720's. [39]

"Detailed use of the *Owanga or wanga,* was used as a very harmful charm. An African by the name of Francois Makandal was also a Haitian Voodoo priest and Maroon leader with many followers. Makandal was also a Muslim who plotted to kill all the whites in San Dominique by poisoning the water supply. "Mackandal created poisons from island herbs. He distributed the poison to slaves, who added it to the meals and refreshments they

---

[39] Hall, Gwendolyn Midlo (1995). Africans in Colonial Louisiana: The Development of Afro-Creole Culture in the Eighteenth Century. Louisiana State University Press. p.162

served the French plantation owners and planters."[40] "Certain documents connected to this investigation revealed detailed information about Voodoo practices. Slaves fastened these *wanga* charms to either the beds or tables of their masters thinking the charms would provide protection from them, making their masters blind to the slaves' faults and therefore soft hearted towards them. It was further explained in these documents that the sorcerers that made these charms made them specifically to poison an enemy or a rival, using the ground up roots of the *figuier maudit tree*. (The *figuier maudit tree* is known as the *evil fig tree*. Because the slaves brought the seeds and the trees to America, they now grow in Florida, Louisiana, Mexico and other tropical climates.) Makandal and other sorcerers pronounced curses over the *wanga* and invoked the name of the Muslim God, Allah as well as the Christian God, Jesus Christ for protection, then finally pronounced, *"God gives me what I do; God gives them that ask."* The manufacture of these charms illustrates the openness of African religious beliefs brought to the Americas; the willingness to invoke the protection of both Islamic and Christian gods and to add them to traditional African beliefs."[41] These 'beliefs' were not only brought into the Catholic

---

[40] Bryan, Patrick E. (1984), The Haitian Revolution and its Effects, ISBN 0-435-98301-6

[41] Hall, Gwendolyn Midlo (1995). Africans in Colonial Louisiana: The Development of Afro-Creole Culture in the Eighteenth Century. Louisiana State University Press. pgs.164,165

religion hundreds of years ago, they were brought into millions of families through the multi-cultural generational iniquity of our ancestors.

Mind blowing, isn't it? You might have the same generational curse originating from Voodoo as a lot of other unsuspecting folks. It never would have occurred to me that was floating around somewhere in my ancestry, but thank GOD He revealed it. Do you know how many people fall into any one of the four categories you just read about, of either Native American, African-American, Muslim or Catholic?

As you can see, there is a strong connection between the African-American community, Catholicism, voodoo and generational curses. Escondido is a city that has many generations rooted in Native American history as well as the Catholic traditions, but this can be true of many families and cities throughout America, depending on the influences that are predominant in each one. Families across America and throughout the world are affected by generational curses – unless they have specifically taken the time and care to investigate their own personal history and renounce them. It's what you don't know about in your family history that can hurt you. How many people would be better off today had they known sooner about the need to renounce generational sin, and therefore tap into the ability to unlock the blessings of God? How many blessings have been held back in your family line that you will never be able to receive *unless* you renounce your sins and those of your ancestors? There is only one way to find out.

God's people perish for lack of knowledge. It's important to clarify certain things about the way we understand certain religious teachings, our own personal history, practices and beliefs. The things people may have accepted as normal and acceptable can produce more bondage and curses, simply because they never knew how the spiritual dynamics worked. The broken areas of people's lives will continue to plague families until they are healed and addressed in such a way that it cuts off demonic attachments associated with that family line.

In the next chapter we will explore more on the subject of spiritually rooted issues so that more of these things become easier to recognize. It takes God's wisdom and revelation to get down to the root of certain problems. May He speak to you and reveal truth as you continue to explore the foundations of your family.

CHAPTER SEVEN
DEMONIC ROOT SYSTEMS

"Even now the axe is laid to the root of the trees. Every tree therefore that does not bear good fruit is cut down and thrown into the fire." Luke 3:9 ESV

All denominations and all groups of faith will be tempted to take an artifact, an icon, or a symbol and turn it into an idol of worship. Sometimes people can also love, admire and respect another individual so much they put them on a pedestal, and that pedestal becomes a form of idolatry. People throughout history have repeatedly shown the weaknesses of their humanity and their failure to keep on the straight ways of the Lord. Israel was God's chosen people and they got it wrong a lot of the time!

In Numbers 21:4-9, the children of Israel had grown tired of trudging through the desert and they were full of complaints. They were discontent with their leader, the provision and the idiosyncrasies of the road map. They were tired of wandering and they grew bitter out of frustration. Then they began to sin with their mouth, complaining against Moses and his God. So, God sent serpents to bite them. Inflicted with deadly poison, they began to die in the wilderness. Then they really began to wail! There is so much that can be said for this passage of scripture and I won't cover it all. It's important to realize that these were a people that had gone through an extremely long, trying wilderness season in their lives. They were worn out. *Done.* Can't take another step, God. What do tired, worn out, frustrated people do? They complain. It seems like an unfair punishment for them to then be punished with snakebite, doesn't it? God wasn't punishing them for being tired or discouraged; He's not that kind of Father. No, the snakes were symbolic of the *rebellion and bitterness* that filled their hearts and caused them to complain against Him. God could have just removed the snakes, but He didn't. Instead, He gave them a remedy for snakebite. We will encounter a lot of problems in life and some may cause us tremendous pain. Instead of removing all our problems, God has graciously provided a remedy for our pain and suffering. He has blessed us with an anti-venom to neutralize the effects of deadly poison. *Jesus.* God told Moses to make a pole with a bronze serpent upon it, and the people were to gaze upon the serpent. If they were obedient, they would live. They were forced to focus upon the results of their sin, and that action brought them to repent. The serpent lifted up upon the pole became symbolic of

Jesus upon the cross.

That symbol of deliverance later became an idol of worship. The people misdirected their faith into a symbol instead of placing their trust in God. This applies to artifacts, icons, symbols of worship and traditions. This would be an example of a religious root of idolatry.

If we truly want to release healing in our families, communities and cities, then we must deal with foundational and spiritually rooted issues. We cannot solve spiritually rooted problems with natural solutions. Addictions, for instance, are rooted in rejection and a need to feel loved, valued and accepted. The root of rejection comes most often from a lack of parental love (a sense of abandonment), acceptance and validation, but sometimes the enemy's lies get so rooted in the person's thought life that they can't get away from the negative voices in their head. It is so important to be able to identify the source of the voices in our head. When a person does not feel loved, they begin to reject themselves, but then they look for ways to fill the void in their heart to compensate for feeling unloved, rejected or unworthy. Those false forms of comfort can end up becoming addictions.

The root of rejection frequently results in sickness and disease. Many physical illnesses and disease, especially autoimmune diseases have their roots in spirits of self-rejection, self-hatred and guilt. ***A 'root issue' refers to a point of origin.*** People often have a spiritually rooted issue develop as a result of some traumatic event in their life. Perhaps their trust was violated, or someone hurt them terribly. Fear comes in as a result of that painful event. If fear is not cast out, eventually it can result in anger or control issues, for fear is the root of both of those emotions. That anger is often either internalized, and the person turns their anger inward upon themselves; or, they turn their anger outward and express it towards others. Either way, those spirits are responsible for toxic emotions and negative behaviors. In order to resolve the behavioral issues, it is imperative that the spiritual issues are properly dealt with through forgiveness, repentance and deliverance.

When a person attacks themselves through self-hatred and self-rejection, the body eventually begins to come into agreement with what is going on spiritually and begins to attack itself. This gives place to a spirit of infirmity. Agreements made in the spiritual realm carry great significance. People that speak words of self-abasement dishonor and disrespect how God created them. Their words are full of unbelief, which forms an agreement with the spirit of death rather than life. The longer it continues, the more that fear, anxiety, illness and other spirits grow stronger. Those things can eventually weaken a person so much they often cannot recover. Repentance and breaking agreement with those negative words are the only way to turn the situation around so that the body can begin to heal. We must break those ungodly covenants that have been made with unbelief. If we don't, unbelief will bind our faith and restrict our ability to grow spiritually.

Grief from personal loss and unhealed wounds from the past can create emotional ties that are used to affect our physical bodies. God's word is a well-spring of wisdom.

"The human spirit can endure in sickness, but a crushed spirit who can bear?" Proverbs 18:14 NIV

"For I am afflicted and needy, And my heart is wounded within me." Psalm 109:22

"A joyful heart is good medicine, But a broken spirit dries up the bones." Proverbs 17:22

This is in no way meant to discourage people from getting medical advice when necessary. We need physicians, but we also need to apply the wisdom of God. I don't believe every single thing has a spiritual root, but many things do as a result of people's sin. Sin has a tendency to be a word that causes people to feel bothered or offended. When people feel that someone else is implying they've done something wrong, they get defensive. It's not my intention to offend anyone by the use of this word; it's just what God calls it. Sin can have several definitions that we have either crossed a moral line and done something wrong; or it can mean that we intentionally did something we knew was wrong. It can also mean having done something that causes us to be estranged from God. Our actions can cause us to either draw closer to God, or result in separation. Isaiah 59:2 and Psalm 66:18-20 tells us that sin causes separation from God and causes Him to hide His face from us. I don't know about you, but in light of that, I don't want God to hide His face from me. I want to know that we are on good terms all the time, and that when I pray, He wants to answer. Therefore, if I want a good relationship with God, then I cannot afford to justify my own faults and erroneous beliefs. It is my responsibility to find out what God has said in His word so that I do not transgress and end up estranged from God.

Do you feel God is distant from you?

Does God answer your prayers?

Do you feel loved, valued and accepted by God?

How you answer those three questions reflects a great deal on whether or not you have something between you and God that needs to be resolved.

In order to live a life of true health and wellness, at least to the best of our ability, then we must take a number of things into consideration. Many physical problems such as illness and disease can be traced back to scripture.

Bitterness is another deeply rooted spirit. The fruit of bitterness is corrupt and will always produce evil. It is very, very difficult to dislodge. I personally struggled with this issue all my life. It was a generational curse passed down through my bloodline. Because of the longevity in our family line, it was very difficult to get free. I suffered from high levels of stress, anger, ulcers, gall bladder pain and a number of digestive issues. There was a period of about 4 years where the chronic pain was so severe on a daily basis that I had a hard time coping. It didn't matter what I ate, or didn't eat. The pain was always there. Most days I felt so depleted that I could not function very well. During this time, God continued to take me into deeper levels of understanding about spiritually rooted issues. He was dealing with core issues of my heart and life. I wrestled for years with that thing but it always came back - *until* I incorporated fasting. Fasting allowed me to finally get free.

Bitterness is not just a feeling or emotion, it is a demonic spirit. That is why it is so important not to make excuses for justifying anger, offense or unforgiveness. Our emotions are real, and sometimes they can be very raw if a person has been hurt. But once toxic emotions grab hold of a person's heart, it can be very difficult to get free. This spiritual root can also cause serious health issues such as ulcers, cancers and gall-bladder disease. Bitter envy, which is under the strongman of jealousy, can cause many harmful effects on the human body, including cancer.

"A peaceful heart leads to a healthy body; jealousy is like cancer in the bones." Prov. 14:30 NLT

Some translations of that scripture use the word envy rather than bitterness. Bitterness is such an important issue to the Lord because it comes from unforgiveness, and holding onto unforgiveness releases a whole host of other problems. First, it is disobedience to the commandments of the Lord to forgive others.

"Bearing with one another and, if one has a complaint against another, forgiving each other; as the Lord has forgiven you, so you also must forgive." Colossians 3:13

"Be kind to one another, tenderhearted, forgiving one another, as God in Christ forgave you." Ephesians 4:32

"For if you forgive others their trespasses, your heavenly Father will also forgive you, but if you do not forgive others their

trespasses, neither will your Father forgive your trespasses." Matthew 6:14,15

Secondly, unforgiveness can turn to bitterness and rebellion, which is tied into witchcraft and idolatry. The Apostle Peter, in Acts 8:23, confronted a sorcerer who wanted to obtain the gift of the Holy Spirit through illegitimate means. Peter challenged him by saying,

"Repent, therefore, of your wickedness, and pray to the Lord. Perhaps He will forgive you for the intent of your heart. For I see that you are poisoned by bitterness and captive to iniquity." Acts 8:23, Berean study Bible

The King James version uses the word "gall" in the above scripture. Gall in this portion of scripture means the essence of bitterness or poison. It has a stupefying effect. It is literally like a drug that intoxicates a person and allows them to be under the influence of another spirit. If a person can't seem to recognize the truth of their own spiritual reality, often God communicates this truth through dreams involving drinking, drug use or addictions. What He is trying to say is, "You are under the influence of a spirit that is not my Holy Spirit." This spirit of stupor literally desensitizes the person that is under the influence and blinds them of their own need to repent. Lying spirits whisper false realities, creating an illusion of deception in the person's mind and heart, keeping them bound to sin and iniquity. Many people get so used to listening to these wrong voices that they mistake them for the voice of God. They then become a channel for that spirit to speak through them. It may even sound like prophecy, but the spirit behind it will cause defilement because the origin is not pure; it's demonic. Confusion, fear or discouragement can set in when words laced with a spirit of death are spoken over us. A spirit of python or pythos which is divination and witchcraft, will also bind a person's faith, vision, and dreams for the future and cause them to feel hopeless, perpetuating the spirit of bitterness. It literally tries to suffocate the life out of the individual.

The sorcerer's sin was wanting the honor and power of an apostle, but he did not care to have the character or disposition of a Christian. Peter discerned that he had a spirit of bitterness about him, and that was deeply connected to his rebellion against the Lord, and his ties to the occult. 1 Samuel 15:23 says,

"Rebellion is as sinful as witchcraft, and stubbornness as bad as worshiping idols." NLT

Now, connect the dots between bitterness and rebellion against God. It is the very root of witchcraft. Do you know what bitter people do? They speak about the things they are bitter about. They rehearse their hurt. They speak word curses against the people and things that they feel are responsible for their hurt, misfortune, or misery in life. The negative energy they feed off of and release into the atmosphere actually releases demonic spirits to carry out curses, sometimes in the lives of those they despise, *but* **the curse always finds its way back to them as well.**

Jesus said the sins you retain are retained, and the sins you remit are remitted.

"If you forgive the sins of any, their sins have been forgiven them; if you retain the sins of any, they have been retained." NASB

If you forgive someone else's sin, they are forgiven, but if you don't forgive, who retains them? You do.

"For if you forgive men their trespasses, your Heavenly Father will also forgive you. but if you do not forgive others their trespasses, neither will your Father forgive your trespasses." Matthew 6:14, 15 ESV

A third problem that results from unforgiveness issues is that it prevents us from inheriting salvation. That's a big one. Because it's such a big deal to God (and should be to us, too), God's mercy allows for us to receive some pretty serious motivation to forgive.

It comes in the form of demonic torment. According to Matthew 18:34, the person who refuses to forgive is turned over to demonic tormentors and is cast into a debtor's prison. They won't be let out until they cry out for deliverance and are willing to repent of their sin. They find themselves in torment; unforgiveness blocks their prayers from being answered, the heavens are silent, they may have long term infirmity and sickness or other health issues, and their thoughts are tormented so they have no peace.[42] I remember ministering to a woman who had numerous health issues, including a lot of back pain, for over 20 years. (Many times back pain can be attributed to alignment issues between ourselves, God and others). I watched as people praying over her tried to release healing. Although a little progress was made, there was obviously something that was resisting her ability to receive her healing. The pastor finally asked if anyone else might have a word for this woman. I went to her and whispered in her ear, "Is there anyone you might need to forgive, even someone from many years ago?" She nodded yes. I asked her if she might be willing to forgive that person and let it go, in light of the fact that it was hindering her ability to be healed. She agreed, and I asked her to very quietly speak it out of her mouth that she forgave that person who had hurt her. Once she did, she began to feel the power of God all over her body. She left feeling immensely better than she came in, all

---

[42] Ref. Isaiah 57:20,21 NKJV

because she found the connection between the root of infirmity and the need to forgive.

Jesus advised those who were weighed down by their burdens and tired from heavy labor to come to him for a divine exchange: give Him the burdens, and take on His yoke. What was His yoke? *Obedience.* Obedience to God is exercising humility, which always defeats the power of the enemy.

"Come to me, all you that labor and are heavy burdened, and I will give you rest." Matthew 11:28, NKJV

A lack of peace is to be agitated, annoyed, discontent, depressed, discouraged, restless, anxious and uneasy. In the book, *A More Excellent Way – Be in Health,* by Henry Wright, the author addresses spiritual roots of disease as separation on one of three levels. It's either separation from ourselves, God or others that creates a lack of peace. A lack of peace is called *dis*-ease.[43] Disease. People may also experience demonic torment attacking their physical bodies in some form of illness or pain. They are subject to a curse. Bitterness puts people under a curse. So many people need deliverance in this area and don't understand why they

---

[43] Wright: A More Excellent Way © 1999, 2000, 2001,2002,2003,2004,2005, Pleasant Valley Publications, Pleasant Valley Church, Inc.

can't seem to make any headway in their prayers. The more bitter and frustrated they get, the angrier they get. Unbelief takes hold of their hearts and they feel abandoned by God. It's a vicious cycle. Unfortunately, as rebellion and unbelief towards God grows stronger, this also means that the power of witchcraft, spiritual poverty and the curse grows stronger in a person's life. Rebellion is the root of witchcraft, and bitterness is another root closely intertwined in it.

When talking about spiritually rooted issues, these are only the tip of the iceberg. There are so many more. Witchcraft is energized by negative emotions and anger. That is why we must do everything possible to purify our hearts and get rid of all unforgiveness, anger, offense, malice and bitterness. Christian or not, if a person operates in a spirit of bitterness and allows that to be released through their prayers or their words to others, *it will attract more demonic spirits.* That is how the enemy reproduces a curse into a person's life. Unforgiveness is a common door the enemy uses to gain access. If he doesn't find a door readily available, all he has to do is create one through a relationship problem. Hurt, anger or offense, if not resolved quickly, can be brushed aside by the individual while the door remains open to the enemy. Some troublesome devil is sent to create the situation that allows a door to be opened, and then he has legal entrance. The only way to shut the door on the enemy and get him out is through repentance.

So many people struggle with unforgiveness and bitterness. What is bound up inside of us causes restriction, constriction and can literally stop the flow of the Holy Spirit in a person's life. When the power of the Holy Spirit is blocked off, the power of resurrection life becomes blocked. Bitterness, anger, strife and unforgiveness are things that will literally shut off the power of God. It is the power of the Holy Spirit that produces strength to overcome any problem. The joy of the Lord is our strength. It is the power of God that needs to be loosed in our life, and in the lives of those we encounter, that will reverse the curse and set people free so that they, too, can experience the goodness of God and worship Him. In the last chapter of the book you will find prayers to break curses and declarations to release transformation and breakthrough. The following are some strategic methods to break demonic power over a family, cities, and throughout our nation.

Strategies to Break Demonic Power

1. The first step to breaking the power of the enemy in a person's life is salvation. Salvation is always the first step, because it is the act of transferring the person out of the kingdom of darkness, into the kingdom of light.

"For he has rescued us from the kingdom of darkness and transferred us into the Kingdom of his dear Son..."Col. 1:13

2. The second step involves inviting the indwelling presence of the Holy Spirit. Invite Him to take the reins of your life. He is our heavenly teacher, helper and interpreter of the Word of God. He is the Spirit of Truth, and it's His job to lead people into all truth. He will help us understand not just the letter of the law, but the spirit in keeping with God's word. We don't benefit from natural wisdom, which is labeled as sensual and filled with demonic influences;[44] we seek after God's wisdom that flows from a Holy source.

"What father among you, if his son asks for a fish, will give him a snake instead? Or if he asks for an egg, will give him a scorpion? So if you who are evil know how to give good gifts to your children, how much more will your Father in heaven give the Holy Spirit to those who ask Him!" Luke 11:12 Berean Study Bible

---

[44] Ref. James 3:16,17

"And if the Spirit of him who raised Jesus from the dead is living in you, he who raised Christ from the dead will also give life to your mortal bodies because of his Spirit who lives in you." Romans 8:11 NIV

3. Understand your identity in Christ. You are loved, valued and accepted through Jesus Christ, who shed His blood for you. When a person understands their identity as a son or daughter of the Most High God, they have a greater ability to discern spiritual truth and walk in love.

"So we praise God for the glorious grace he has poured out on us who belong to his dear Son." Ephesians 1:6 NIV

"Therefore, if anyone is in Christ, he is a new creation. The old has passed away; behold, the new has come." 2 Cor. 5:17 ESV

4. Exercise dominion over the enemy. Jesus transferred all authority over to His disciples. We have been given power over the enemy.

"I have given you authority to trample on snakes and scorpions and to overcome all the power of the enemy; nothing will harm you." Luke 10:19 NIV

Then God said, "Let Us make man in Our image, according to Our likeness; and let them rule over the fish of the sea and over the birds of the sky and over the cattle and over all the earth, and over every creeping thing that creeps on the earth." Genesis 1:26

"You make him to rule over the works of Your hands; You have put all things under his feet," Psalm 8:6

5. Right alignment with God and others. Broken relationships create stress, guilt, fear and anxiety. Those things cause a lack of confidence towards God until the conscience is cleansed of guilt. As much as possible, live at peace with others and so what you can to heal broken relationships.

"And by this we will know that we belong to the truth, and will assure our hearts in His presence: If our hearts condemn us, God is greater than our hearts, and He knows all things. Beloved, if our hearts do not condemn us, we have confidence before God,..." 1 John 3:19-21, Berean Study Bible

"If we claim to be without sin, we deceive ourselves and the truth is not in us. If we confess our sins, he is faithful

and just and will forgive us our sins and purify us from all unrighteousness." 1 John 1:8,9 NIV

6. Obedience. Jesus was obedient in all things, and as a result, he could say that the 'ruler of this world' could find nothing in him to exploit.

"I don't have much more time to talk to you, because the ruler of this world approaches. He has no power over me" John 14:30 NLT

7. Operate in love and humility. The common denominator in all demonic spirits is rebellion created by pride. If we want to overcome all the power of evil, we must operate in the opposite spirit.

"Do not be overcome by evil, but overcome evil with good." Rom. 12:21 NIV

"Do not repay evil with evil or insult with insult. On the contrary, repay evil with blessing, because to this you were called so that you may inherit a blessing." 1 Peter 3:9 NIV

8. Speak life. The word of god is full of power. It contains

the power to break the demonic grip and loose individuals into a new cycle.

"For the word of God is alive and active. Sharper than any double-edged sword, it penetrates even to dividing soul and spirit, joints and marrow; it judges the thoughts and attitudes of the heart." Heb. 4:12 NIV

"The tongue has the power of life and death, and those who love it will eat its fruit." Prov. 18:21

"For by your words you will be acquitted, and by your words you will be condemned." Matthew 12:37

9. Don't just try to treat the fruit; look for the root. Refer to the chart on the strongmen. If you don't take the axe to the root, the bad fruit will always come back. Jesus cursed the fruitless fig tree and commanded it to bear no more fruit. We can do the same to those bad trees with evil roots. Jesus also told us that good trees cannot bear bad fruit, and that we would know false brethren 'by their fruit.' Bad fruit is evidence of something growing off of a demonic root, at least a great deal of the time. Break off your sins with righteousness. They produce good fruit. Good fruit helps to produce a new cycle in life where God releases His blessings. Declare a new root system.

"Seeing a fig tree by the road, he went up to it but found nothing on it except leaves. Then he said to it, "May you never bear fruit again!" Immediately the tree withered. Matthew 21:19

"He will be like a tree firmly planted by streams of water, Which yields its fruit in its season And its leaf does not wither; And in whatever he does, he prospers." Ps. 1:3

10. Release prophetic words. Prophetic evangelism is sharing with others, by the unction of the Holy Spirit, what God says about them. Those anointed words often have the power to completely shift the direction of a person's life. Look at all the biblical examples of when Jesus called His disciples: They responded to the call and immediately changed direction in their lives. Saul, who experienced a dramatic conversion upon an unexpected meeting with the Spirit of Jesus, had a life changing encounter and became a different person. They suddenly become aware that God has a different (better) plan for their lives than where they've been living, and the good news has the power to shift them in the direction of God's will for their life. I know from experience that was true for me, as it is for many others. Many people who seem to be wandering in

life or living a life of sin are simply lost and discouraged. They don't have a road map and they don't know their purpose. When purpose is clarified, and when the answers to the questions of their heart calm their troubled minds, they often gain the inner strength and conviction to change course.

11. Release prophetic decrees that utilize the word of God. The scriptures are anointed to produce exactly what God has purposed they will do, whether it is physical healing, tearing down strongholds, unraveling demonic plans or tearing up demonic root systems.

"Is not My word like fire?" declares the LORD, "and like a hammer which shatters a rock?" Jer. 23:29

"Today I appoint you to stand up against nations and kingdoms. Some you must uproot and tear down, destroy and overthrow. Others you must build up and plant." Jeremiah 1:10 NIV

"At one moment I might speak concerning a nation or concerning a kingdom to uproot, to pull down, or to destroy it;" Jeremiah 18:7 NIV

"As I have watched over them to pluck up, to break down, to overthrow, to destroy and to bring disaster, so I will watch over them to build and to plant," declares the LORD." Jeremiah 31:28 NIV

"It is the same with my word. I send it out, and it always produces fruit. It will accomplish all I want it to, and it will prosper everywhere I send it." Isaiah 55:11 NLT

12. Confess your sins to God, and to one another that you may be healed. Confession works on several levels. The first thing is does is demonstrate humility. Humility is the trump card over the works of the devil. We can take responsibility for our own sins and those of our ancestors by being very thorough and honest about ourselves and our family history. Second, confession between ourselves and someone we trust helps us enter into an even deeper level of humility. It is bearing our soul in honesty to another human being, acknowledging our need to ask someone else to pray for us. God designed the members of His body to need one another and receive from one another. Trusting His method shows dependence upon Him and others, and allows us to become a recipient of the divine grace that heals.

"Therefore confess your sins to each other and pray for each other so that you may be healed. The prayer of a righteous person is powerful and effective." James 5:16 NIV

Read the story of Hilkiah the high priest and King Josiah in 2 Kings 22:22-23:25. It's an amazing story of repentance, rival and restoration. The people confessed their sin and revival came upon the land. God's blessing came upon His people.

13. Fasting. Fasting has the power to humble our flesh, allowing our spirit man to take the dominant role. Fasting allows us to focus on God and subdue other appetites so that we can hear from God. Some spirits will only be dislodged through the added component of fasting along with prayer. Saturate your heart in worship while fasting for a few days. Our hearts are like soil. If the ground is dry and caked, it would be very difficult to pull out a stubborn weed with a long root. Worship allows the soil of our heart to become pliable and less resistant so that when God speaks, we are more apt to obey. It will almost always involve repentance and confession of sin on some level. What God is looking for is genuine softening of our heart towards our own sin, and perhaps our attitude towards

forgiving others, too. When the soil of our heart is well saturated and Holy Spirit speaks as to the root of our issue, the root will come out much easier.

"And he said unto them, This kind can come forth by nothing, but by prayer and fasting." Mark 9:29 KJV

14. Cleanse your home/land/property of things that may be associated with a curse. Certain things such as tribal masks, obelisks, Buddha statues, idols, prayer books from other religions, New Age objects such as crystals, incense, tarot cards, Masonic Handbooks and books from other secret societies are examples of things that are cursed objects. Even some forms of music invite a demonic presence. Remove them and burn them. Then speak over your home and say, "In the name and authority of the Lord Jesus Christ, I command every unclean, evil spirit to leave these premises immediately. I divorce you and break every covenant that has been made knowingly or unknowingly by myself or my ancestors. You are not wanted nor allowed in this home and I command you to leave now. Go back to where you came from in Jesus name. Amen."

"Many who had believed now came forward, confessing and disclosing their deeds. And a number of those who had practiced magic arts brought their books and burned them in

front of everyone. When the value of the books was calculated, it came to fifty thousand drachmas." Acts 19:18-19 Berean Study Bible

CHAPTER EIGHT

COMMITTING TO SPIRITUAL GROWTH

"But solid food is for the mature, who by constant use have trained their sensibilities to distinguish good from evil." Hebrews 5:14

It is unfortunate but there are many Christians that are reluctant, and even stubborn about entering into new levels of spiritual growth and understanding. Some of that comes with an improper foundation of teaching, but some of it is just pride. We cannot afford to believe that we have all that is needed in our spiritual education. A wise person continues to seek after God and grow in their relationship with Him.

If you are employed and your boss asks you to take some specialized classes in order to help you become a better, more effective employee and you refused, how long do you think you would last? A lack of commitment to learn and grow with your company would hurt your ability to advance and earn promotions.

It might even get you fired. It would seem ridiculous, as well as presumptuous, to believe that you might be given a big promotion even though you refused the free classes that your boss offered, in hopes that you would become a better asset to the company. Who is going to get the promotion, the raise and increase in company benefits? The guy who readily showed his commitment to advancing the goals of the organization.

The body of Christ is a huge spiritual organization and our Father is serious about advancing His kingdom. In the same way, we must understand how adopting an attitude that resists spiritual education and growth can hurt us in a myriad of ways. This is why God gives us teachers, to give us spiritual understanding so that we can achieve greater levels of personal growth. We can remain trapped in negative cycles that perpetuate loss, poverty, brokenness, disappointment and leave us utterly stuck in frustration, all because we refused to acknowledge our own need to adjust our perspective. God resists the proud, but gives grace to the humble. He has a better, more excellent way to overcome the powers of evil.

In a more personal perspective, think of your relationship with Jesus as a marriage. If you didn't involve your spouse in any of your decisions, how do you think they would feel? If you didn't say good morning, or kiss them goodnight, or go out of your way to show your love to them, would you really be holding up your end of your vows? Do you want to have great conversation with your spouse? Do you want to know what pleases him/her in order to have a better relationship? Well, of course you would. It would be silly not to, right? Growing in our love relationship with God is the same way. It take nurturing and care to grow a great relationship.

Having a relationship with Jesus isn't just about following a set of rules. It's about love and commitment. As in any love relationship, it might be difficult to pin point exactly when our spouse had our whole heart – but when we continued dating long enough, it just naturally happened. It's like that with our relationship with God, too. Just stay in the relationship. Sooner or later you'll realize He won your heart, because you already won His. He is madly in love with you!

Our heavenly Father is continually releasing fresh insights, wisdom, understanding and strategies if we will just listen and obey His directives. He is constantly in the business of giving us upgrades in our ability to strategize with Him. In order to effectively utilize the secrets He shares with us, we must be willing to learn from our Teacher, and from the teachers He places in our lives. This is how we know what weapons to use in any given season. The Commander of the Angel Armies, and our Anointed

King works with us to help us overcome every tactic of the enemy's spiritual warfare. Our willingness to continue to learn and sharpen the skills of our prayer life and ministry continues until we have finished the good fight of faith and we are taken home. I pray that you approach your relationship to God with an open mind and a heart that is committed to spiritual growth.

"I keep asking that the God of our Lord Jesus Christ, the glorious Father, may give you the Spirit of wisdom and revelation, so that you may know him better. I pray that the eyes of your heart may be enlightened in order that you may know the hope to which he has called you..." Eph. 1:17,18 NIV

CHAPTER NINE
THE POWER OF THE DECREE

"And you will also decree a thing, and it will be established for you, and light will shine on your ways." Job 22:28

One thing that I have learned is a crucial component of prayer is to utilize the word of God. When I was younger in the Lord I did not see the value of praying the word of God. I didn't want to be responsible for learning scripture or devoting myself to prayer. Unfortunately, that resistance was simply pride, and pride never gets us very far. I felt like my prayers were wandering all over the place like a drunk staggering out of the local bar. I didn't know what to pray or how to make sure I was actually accomplishing anything with my prayers. I also didn't see the kind of results I wanted to get out of prayer. An elder had told me to pray like Jesus did, returning the word of God to Him in my prayers. At the time, I felt like this person was just a religious fanatic, and I didn't want to turn out like her, so I didn't take her advice. After experiencing what felt like a brick wall when it came to my prayer life, I decided to try her suggestion. I found that my prayers began to be answered and it greatly encouraged me to continue in that manner.

I have seen God do some amazing things because I was willing to dig through His word and proclaim it in faith. When Jesus was tempted in the wilderness, He fought the devil by only speaking the word of God. He rebuked Satan with scripture, but He also demonstrated what it was to return the word of the law to His Father in faith, knowing the word of God held power to defeat his adversary.

One powerful tool to combat the enemy is to write and declare prayer declarations. In the book of Esther, Queen Esther found herself as well as her people (the Jews) threatened with annihilation. A very treacherous man named Haman, who happened to be her husband's right hand man and advisor, had unscrupulously written a decree that meant the destruction of her people. The king signed the decree, not understanding that he had literally just signed his own wife's death warrant; but, at that time, nothing could undo the word of a king. The king was furious with Haman, and Haman feared for his life. Rightfully so! That guy was toast. He met his end pretty quickly, but there was still the matter of the death warrant that went out all across the land, notifying the Jews that on a certain date they would be exterminated. At Esther's appeal, the king suddenly had a bright idea. Esther could write a new decree! And so she did. Queen Esther wrote a new decree, advising all the Jews that on the day that was scheduled for their destruction, they were to rise up and defend themselves and annihilate the forces of anyone that would try to assault them or plunder their possessions.

"You yourselves write a decree concerning the Jews, just as you please, in the king's name and seal it with the king's signet ring: for whatever is written in the king's name and sealed with the king's signet ring no one can revoke." Esther 8:8

As in all wonderful stories, a miraculous turn-around occurred just in the nick of time, and the Jews were saved - all because a woman dared to step out in faith and petition the king for a favor. Esther's king couldn't say no; he adored her! Our king won't say no to us either; He adores us! So write your decrees, and turn the tables on the enemy. Do you see a problem that needs fixing? Are you sick and tired of the enemy having the upper hand? Do you have a problem in your community, city, state or nation? Write a new decree!

Intent is everything when it comes to prayer. The first thing one needs to understand about writing a decree is the importance of truly understanding the Father's heart. God's heart is full of longsuffering and lovingkindness, but it is balanced with judgment against the works of darkness and evil. Justice cannot exist unless judgment is executed against acts of injustice, treachery and oppression. Jesus came to set the captives free! His mercy and perfect loving nature insures that He is the final determining factor in how His word is fulfilled. It is our responsibility to declare His will in the earth. It's not enough to declare His word without passion. We must speak in such a way that it reflects His heart and the qualities of His character towards others.

"Thus says the Lord, "Let not the one who is wise and skillful boast in his insight; let not the one who is mighty and powerful boast in his strength; let not the one who is rich boast in his [temporal satisfactions and earthly] abundance; but let the one who boasts boast in this, that he understands and knows Me [and acknowledges Me and honors Me as God and recognizes without any doubt], that I am the Lord who practices lovingkindness, justice and righteousness on the earth, for in these things I delight," says the Lord. (Jeremiah 9:23,24 AMP)

Every person must be able to assess the motive behind their own words. There are many intercessors that bring their own personal judgments into their prayers and they pray out of a soulish level. This is very dangerous. The spirit realm knows and understands when a person is operating out of a soulish level and their words are energized by negative emotions such as offense, anger, a desire for judgment, vengeance or an unloving spirit. It is very important for the individual to realize if their heart is in need of healing because it's very possible to release a spirit of witchcraft. The very basis of witchcraft is that a person's will and emotion are the driving force behind their words. They speak with the intent to will certain things to come to pass. They may or may not realize they are doing it, but they are trying to force their will to come to pass, rather than yielding to Holy Spirit and praying His will into a situation. Operating in a spirit of witchcraft opens the door for witchcraft attacks to boomerang back into the life of the one that sends out those words. It is also important to take precautions such as deep cleansing prayer prior to engaging in spiritual warfare. Many, many people go into spiritual warfare ill prepared. They have unbroken generational curses or other open doors that the enemy will use to exploit an area of weakness. Devils looks for our blind spot; an open door we don't realize is there. It is wisdom to make sure that one doesn't engage the enemy when they could have open doors that grant him access to their lives. These type of precautions limit the enemy's ability to retaliate and protect those that are attempting to enforce kingdom laws.

Decrees are written to execute judgment against the works of evil, release people from bondage, overturn injustice, tear down ungodly authority structures, tear up faulty foundations and evict the enemy. Decrees also help plant new ministries, lay the correct foundation, realign, restructure, revive and restore. They bring forth justice for the oppressed, route the enemy, establish boundaries, and open the heavens so that kingdom plans and purposes can move forward. They make room for the ground troops to advance. Decrees propel and establish kingdom authority.

The first thing I do when writing a new decree is to consider what sort of hindrances need to be dealt with. Identify and address particular obstacles, then I sit down and pray, asking Holy Spirit to help guide me as I write. Effectively enforcing the law of God means that we need to be confident in knowing His will for the situation. His will always reflects a balance of justice with mercy.

A decree or prayer declaration serves several purposes. The first is to state a problematic situation that recognizes the current condition requires necessary action to remedy it. The second is to serve as an indictment that brings lawful charges against the enemy, and the third is to declare what the law states.

Scripture is used to support and declare God's word (the law) that we choose to enforce. I often use the internet to search a key phrase or a thought to bring up a variety of scriptures that will be useful. I also look for various translations that reflect the heart and intent of what I feel needs to be incorporated into the decree. When I first started writing decrees, it took a bit longer to figure out what I wanted them to say, but with practice anyone can write them like a pro. You can too!

What situation do you have in your life or in the life of a family member that needs to be reversed? What injustice needs to overturned? What enemy needs to be captured and hauled into court? Write a new decree. Don't allow the enemy's plots and schemes to stand unchallenged. Decrees engrave the words of God into the situation in the Spirit. Declare His will over your life, family, and your future. Write a new decree over your city, your state and your nation. Overturn injustice! Overthrow corruption! Route the enemy and force him to go where he can be captured and contained. Enforce justice and righteousness by declaring what God has said in His word! The Spirit of the living God resides within you to create, enforce, and establish God's will on earth. We are not victims, we are victorious!

Declaring God's law is to remind Him (and the court of heaven) that action is necessary in order to correct the situation. Therefore, we are calling upon the One who gave us His law and asking that He help us enforce it in the earthly realm. The enemy is a legalist, a thief, the fraudulent witness, the prosecuting attorney (the accuser of the brethren) and a murderer. He is well acquainted with the court of heaven, and he knows how to work the system. He looks for loopholes. It's our job, through our prayers and declarations, to sew up every little area where the enemy might try to wiggle through. It pays to be thorough. We cannot afford to pray haphazardly, throwing out prayers like buckshot, hoping to hit something. We need strategic, well aimed prayers that hit the target every time. Decrees are like a sniper rifle that finds its mark. They are lethal!

Scripture tells us that our true identity lies in the knowledge that we are children of God, and as sons and daughters of the Most High God, we also attain the status of an heir.

'Because you are sons, God has sent forth the Spirit of His Son into our hearts, crying, "Abba! Father!" So you are no longer a slave, but God's child; and since you are his child, God has made you also an heir.' (Galatians 4:6,7 NIV)

But, that's not all… We are also royalty. The word of God tells us so.

'And hath made us kings and priests unto God and his Father; to him be glory and dominion for ever and ever. Amen.' (Rev. 1:6 KJV)

'You have made them to be a kingdom and priests to serve our God, and they will reign on the earth."' (Revelation 5:10 NIV)

Only a person that has been granted authority has the power to reign and establish the dominion of the king. When we become 'born again' into the kingdom of God, we inherit the birthright of an heir to all the kingdom. This knowledge is vital to our understanding who we are in Christ so that we can then live in that reality. Every born again believer wears a crown in the Spirit. The privilege of leadership and authority is granted without us even having to request it.

"I have given you authority to trample on snakes and scorpions and to overcome all the power of the enemy; nothing will harm you." (Luke 10:19 NIV)

Snakes and scorpions are references to all manner of evil. Jesus empowered us to take authority over the works of darkness. It is our responsibility to overturn the works of the enemy. We are empowered with the right to rule and enforce the laws of the Kingdom of God. It is, after all, our homeland. We are citizens of the Kingdom of Heaven. The kingdom and everything in it belongs to us! That is why we, God's people, are referred to as an extension of His authority. We become that royal scepter of authority in our Father's hand, as we legislate the laws of our kingdom, enforcing them 'on earth as it is in heaven.' We rule in the midst of our enemies.

"You will be a crown of splendor in the LORD's hand, a royal diadem in the hand of your God."(Isaiah 62:3 NIV)

"Your throne, O God, will last for ever and ever; a scepter of justice will be the scepter of your kingdom." (Psalm 45:6 NIV)

"The LORD will extend your mighty scepter from Zion, saying, "Rule in the midst of your enemies!" (Psalm 110:2 NIV)

Kings rule by decree. Whether the words are spoken out of their mouth or written in the form of a decree (and then proclaimed to others), the words of a royal ruler are received as law.

There is something we will all benefit from if we commit this to memory: The enemy may not want to obey us, however, there is one thing that Satan must always obey and that is the word of God. When Jesus fought Satan in the wilderness He always responded with "It is written…" and then He would quote scripture. Satan had no choice but to do what Jesus commanded.

Jesus is the living word of God. As the word of God, He is the final authority. Spiritual laws are encoded into every letter of scripture. That is why it is written,

"My word, which comes from my mouth, is like the rain and snow. It will not come back to me without results. It will accomplish whatever I want and achieve whatever I send it to do." (Isaiah 55:11 God's Word Translation).

When we return God's word to Him, angels are released to carry out the fulfillment of the scripture.

"Praise the LORD, you angels of his, you powerful warriors who carry out his decrees and obey his orders!" (Psalm 103:20 NET Bible).

Other translations of this scripture declare that angels both listen for His word and are responsible for executing scripture according to the way He intends the word to be fulfilled. If we want our prayers and declarations to be successful, it is vitally important to utilize the word of God. Sounds waves send out a ripple effect into the atmosphere and the spiritual realm. Those sound waves do not diminish, but remain in the environment where they are sent out. The power of our words create boundaries and barricades against enemy activity.

Decrees are like stealth bombers dropping air strikes over

enemy territory. Stealth aircraft are specifically designed to carry out assignments in secrecy and be able to go through impenetrable enemy defenses. They are designed to travel extremely fast in order to be able to intercept the enemy and catch them by surprise. Stealth bombers have an incredible ability to carry out long range strikes and remain virtually undetectable by radar. Decrees function in the same way and create breakthrough in both the spiritual and earthly realms. The enemy literally has no ability to anticipate the decrees that will be spoken and thus has no capacity to formulate a plan for a counter attack. He doesn't know what will be spoken or where they are going to hit. Decrees send the enemy into fear and confusion. The more God's people incorporate the proper use of scripture into their prayers and declarations, the more power they release to interrupt evil plans and destroy the works of darkness. Do you want power released when you pray? **Decree God's word.**

"You will also decree a thing, and it will be established for you; And light will shine on your ways." (Job 22:28 NASB).

You are the extension of God's authority. Rule in the midst of your enemies!

CHAPTER TEN

A NEW FORM

"The people of the city said to Elisha, "Look, our lord, this town is well situated, as you can see, but the water is bad and the land is unproductive." 2 kings 2:19-22

The men of a certain city approached the prophet Elisha about a problem they didn't know how to resolve. They were quick to point out the city had some positive attributes, but they didn't know what to do about the fact that the ground was unproductive. *Barren.* Nothing would grow.

God's blessing on agriculture is given in Genesis 1:29 where He said that He gave us plants yielding seed for food. Then He gave us a promise that He would water the land so that it would yield it's fruit and the increase – *but,* it was contingent upon obedience.

"And if you will indeed obey my commandments that I command you today, to love the Lord your God, and to serve him with all your heart and with all your soul, he will give the rain for your land in its season, the early rain and the later rain, that you may gather in your grain and your wine and your oil. And he will give grass in your fields for your livestock, and you shall eat and be full." Deut. 11:13-15

There are many references in scripture as to either the blessing or the curse resting on the land and how it affected agriculture. When nothing will grow, it is evidence of a curse. When the heavens are like brass and it doesn't rain for extended periods of time, it's because God wants our attention. There's something blocking the heavens.

"The skies above will be as unyielding as bronze, and the earth beneath will be as hard as iron." Deut. 28:23

"Therefore, because of you the sky has withheld its dew and the earth has withheld its produce." Haggai 1:10

2 Chronicles 6:21-31 also reveals that brass heavens, famine and poor agriculture were the result of disobedience to God. They were afflicted until they turned back to God and confessed their sin.

In many other places in scripture the prophets were sent to a people with a message of judgment unless they repented. However, in this scripture that is not mentioned. God had a different strategy for healing the city. What I find interesting about this scripture in 2 Kings 2:19-22 is the fact that this portion of scripture clearly states that they went *to the source* of the water system. The source of the water system wasn't just the distribution center for the city; it was the root of the problem.

When a river dries up, it becomes a stream, and when a stream dries up, it becomes the breeding ground for spiritual parasites. The water is no longer fit for consumption and can cause sickness and disease. Something else leaks out, defiling the whole water source. Spiritually speaking, it's the same process. Where there is no revelation from the Holy Spirit, where the gifts of the Spirit are not flowing, the spiritual climate becomes stagnant and filled with other influences. Defilement sets in. If we want our cities to have the blessing on agriculture as well as the evidence of other things, it becomes imperative that spiritual wells flow with the living water that Jesus promised in John 7:37-39. Out of this well flows living water that is healing to the nations because it contains the gifts of His Spirit. Jesus told us to long for this life giving drink of water and He would give it as His gift.

"If you only knew the gift God has for you and who you are speaking to, you would ask me, and I would give you living water." John 4:10 NIV

"Whoever believes in me, as Scripture has said, rivers of living water will flow from within them." John 7:38 NIV

"For I will pour out water on the thirsty land And streams on the dry ground; I will pour out My Spirit on your offspring And My blessing on your descendants;" Isaiah 44:3

"It will come about that every living creature which swarms in every place where the river goes, will live. And there will be very many fish, for these waters go there and the others become fresh; so everything will live where the river goes." Ezekiel 47:9

A pure river of life, clear as crystal, proceeds from the throne of God. This river is likened to the Holy Spirit, who longs to fill us with Himself. We can't effectively love others without Him loving through us. I really believe that part of the curse, or maybe all of it, that Elisha encountered in that little city was due to a lack of love. Love is what heals. Love is the source of our power. Love births miracles. All our good efforts fail without it.

Jesus rebuked the Laodicean church with the threat of spewing them out of his mouth because they were indifferent towards Him. Remember, when God sees a city, He sees the *entire body of Christ* in the city. He was tired of their apathy from self-sufficiency. Their pride, arrogance and lack of concern for anyone but themselves was enough to make Him sick. He threatened to vomit them out of His mouth!

**If indifference breeds apathy,
then compassion is the remedy.**

Jesus was moved with compassion when He saw people who were hurting, grieving, tormented and in bondage.

"When he saw the crowds, he had compassion for them, because they were harassed and helpless, like sheep without a shepherd." Matthew 9:36

"Jesus had compassion on them and touched their eyes. Immediately they received their sight and followed him." Matt. 20:34

"And when he drew near and saw the city, he wept over it, saying, "Would that you, even you, had known on this day the things that make for peace! But now they are hidden from your eyes." Luke 19:41,42

Jesus wept over those who would reject Him, but He was full of compassion nevertheless. He never stopped trying to connect with those that were within His reach. It was His compassion that allowed love, grace and anointing to flow out of Him, and where ever He went, people experienced the power of His touch. Miracles are birthed when people move outside of their own comforts and extend themselves to touch others with the love of God.

Elisha took the men of the city to the source of the problem and said, *"Give me a new bowl."* He needed something fresh, something that had no trace of being previously used or could contain anything that would defile what he was about to pour in. Then he asked for salt, because salt was a preservative and an agent for healing. When he threw the salt from the bowl into the source of the water, it purified it and healed it all the way through.

Jesus likened us to salt and light that should impact society with the influence of His kingdom.

"You are the salt of the earth. But if the salt loses its saltiness, how

can it be made salty again? It is no longer good for anything, except to be thrown out and trampled underfoot." Matt. 5:13 NIV

When the body of Christ moves out of the church and into their communities they begin to purify the waters of their community. Christ sent us out to share our lives, our testimonies and the grace of God with others, and in the process we release healing to others. It's not as intimidating as you might think. I've had more spontaneous divine appointments in parking lots and grocery stores than probably anywhere else, you just have to make yourself available!

When God's people step out to touch others, what was once a community or city filled with bitterness, anger, fear and frustration becomes a place known for its compassion. What was once barren and unproductive becomes fruitful and receives the blessing of God. It becomes a place where people find rest from their burdens and the grace of God rains down.

When I think of Elisha telling the people of the city to get a new bowl, he was telling them a new form was what was needed at the moment. The new form isn't tainted by a religious spirit. God has done an incredible work in and through the body of Christ. The church in San Diego county (and I'm sure many other places, too) are actively out there in their communities and excited about hanging out with Jesus, praying for people and sharing what God is saying about them. They're delighting themselves in Him and He is changing the spiritual atmosphere, doing healing miracles and having a really good time! The new wine of His Spirit is being poured out, releasing joy in dry places. Rivers of living water are starting to flow into the streets and communities. Holy Spirit has changed the flavor of the messages coming forth, and changed many hearts in the process. People now understand the importance of integrating with the unchurched in their communities and are actively looking for ways to connect with them like the church at large has not done in a long time. That in itself is wonderful news! God's people are not just the salt and light; they have become the new wine that God is pouring out so that others can taste and see *the Lord is good.*

People have a hard time adjusting to change, and when they cannot bring themselves to make the changes that are necessary, God will bring a variety of circumstances that will force people out of the old form. Just as the act of a mother giving birth forces a child out of the womb and into the world, so it is with us. The mother (the church) must give birth and force her children out of their comfort zone and into the world.

We cannot remain the same, and we cannot remain stuck inside an old form. There are many things coming in the days ahead and God is trying to prepare us now to accept and adapt to the necessary changes. It's a new day. Labor and delivery can be messy and difficult, but the mother cannot try to stop the birth. If she refuses to push the child out of the womb it can kill her and the child. This is not a time to get stuck in religious traditions or man-made restrictions that keep people overly dependent upon religious structures, expectations and constraints. Holy Spirit is responsible for bringing people into maturity. You trust Him to lead you through your own processes; You can also trust Him with other people's processes.

There will always be a need for leadership, guidance, prayer, teaching and equipping but it needs to be brought out into the communities rather than holding on to traditional expectations, wanting people to go find what we typically define as a local church. Our verbiage and our concept must change, too. The church is not the building. *We* are the church, and as such, we steward what God has given us and share those things with others so that they can benefit, too. We are the loaves and fishes that are broken and distributed to feed others.

God's leaders will always lead. A person's true calling is contained in their gifting, character, heart and attitude towards others. It shapes *who* they are regardless of *where* they are. A pastoral calling doesn't go away even when the form changes. A prophetic voice isn't silenced when the church empties out into the streets; the voice just finds a new place to release the words of God. And so it is with all the gifts. They must find a place to impact others. The gifts, callings and mantles are not dependent upon being contained in the old form. It is a time to trust in the Lord for the new. It's time for new places and new faces!

Often, in times of change, we must remember that something needs to die in order for the new to come. Letting go and letting something die is a painful process, but joy comes in the morning as God honors the act of letting go and trusting Him to give us His promise. He longs to give us a gracious provision for a new beginning! It's a time of letting go and trusting God. Old forms are melting away. The walls that once kept people stuck in the old wineskin are disintegrating. A true apostolic mandate is to send people out to do the works of God. In that sense, we are ALL SENT ONES. It is time to help others fulfill their dreams and calling. Ask yourself how you can help others achieve their God-given assignments. Ask yourself how you can help connect them with those that may be divine connections for them. Pray God would do for others the way you want Him to do for you. Ask for new alignments. Send them out with blessing! Send them out so that they can birth what God has given them as their assignment! It's time for the body to arise and shine!

CHAPTER ELEVEN
PRAYERS AND DECLARATIONS
FOR TRANSFORMATION AND BREAKTHROUGH

BREAKTHROUGH PRAYER: Due to the length of this Prayer, sub-headings have been provided. However, it is recommended to pray the whole prayer, not just sections of it. Remember, reading through it is not the same as praying it out of your mouth. This needs to proclaimed out loud.

Initial Declaration

Right now I declare that I break every agreement with Satan and the works of darkness. I choose this day to divorce the enemy, to renounce and repent of any covenants that have been made by myself or other family members in my generational line.

According to YOUR word in 2 Chronicles 7:14, I address:

Spirits of Fear & Self-Condemnation

Whether I or other family members have partaken of these sins knowingly or unknowingly, Father, I ask Your forgiveness and I renounce:

All spirits of fear, the fear of man that brings a snare, self-pity, insecurity, and inferiority.

Forgive those in my family line for the need to control or manipulate others out of a sense of fear, insecurity or inferiority.

Forgive us for not trusting in your provision or your timing, and for failing to rest in Your love.

I renounce all spirits of heaviness that bring depression, mental illness, obsessive compulsive disorders, schizophrenia, suicide, and grief.

I renounce the spirits of unbelief, double-mindedness, the cares of this world and all things that would give me give me divided loyalties in my heart and mind towards God.

I renounce every seed that Satan has sown into my heart and mind that would cause divided loyalties and weaken my convictions towards Jesus Christ.

I renounce bi-polar disease and unbelief.

I renounce all compulsive behavior and all addictions rooted in fear, rejection, or anxiety.

I renounce self-pity and the lie that I cannot or will not be healed.

I renounce the tendency to think of myself as a victim or a martyr in these forms of mental illness.

Father, You love me and did not give me sickness, disease, torment or problems. Those came from the pit of hell. Jesus died for this truth and I will not reject Your truth.

I reject the lies from the enemy and declare that I receive the truth and the healing that is afforded to me as a child of God, for it is written, "By His stripes, I AM healed," in Jesus name.

Spirits of Discontent & Complaining

I renounce and forsake all spirits of discontent, complaining, a vagabond spirit, wandering and irresponsibility that have come from iniquity and idolatry.

I renounce and forsake any sins and demonic spirits associated with gambling, poverty spirits, laziness and sins of poor stewardship.

I renounce all addictive behaviors given to excess, greed or stinginess.

Spirits of Bitterness and Anger

I renounce bitterness, jealousy, strife, anger, hatred, profanity, gossip, lying, slander and murder.

I renounce bitter root judgments that come from being hurt or mistreated, or injustice that has occurred towards myself or others in my family.

I renounce the spirit of Cain, which is a murderous spirit.

I repent and forsake the sins of slander, hatred and evil speaking. I repent of my judgments against others.

Forgive me and those in my family for any sins of hard heartedness, being critical or condemning, or showing lack of compassion towards others in their time of need.

Forgive me and those in my family line for turning a blind eye towards those in need and withholding good when it was in our power to help.

Unforgiveness

I renounce and forsake unforgiveness, including unforgiveness towards myself, retaliation, and vengeance.

Forgive me, LORD, for any time that me or my family members have sown seeds of discord or caused pain to others through our actions.

Forgive us for acts of maliciousness or things that myself or other family members have done with the intent to hurt and cause pain to others.

Forgive me and those in my family line for selective obedience or ignoring the prompting of your Holy Spirit when You wanted us to show love, mercy, grace or compassion.

Pride and Rebellion

I renounce and forsake the sins of pride, lawlessness, rebellion, selfish ambition, presumption, and testing God.

I renounce and forsake atheism, mockery, scoffing the things of God and Your Holy Spirit, grieving the Holy Spirit and unbelief.

Forgive me LORD, for allowing spirits of inferiority or insecurity to drive me to feel as though I have to prove myself to others, myself or to You.

Forgive me for believing these lying spirits when they tried to form a false image in me. Your word says I am fearfully and wonderfully made, and I am made in Your image. I am accepted just as I am.

Forgive me and my family line for despising godly wisdom and authority or rejecting Your counsel.

Forgive us for self-rule and choosing authority figures that did not represent Your government or authority for our lives.

I repent from any time that I have cursed God or others.

Forgive me LORD, for loving gossip, slander and my judgments more than I loved your law of showing love and kindness.

Forgive me for not blessing others more freely, even those I do not like or those that have been an enemy.

Illegitimate Spiritual Relationships

I renounce and forsake all soul ties to illegitimate spiritual fathers or spiritual leaders, religious attitudes, and spirits of legalism, disrespect, self-righteousness, prejudice, controlling behaviors, manipulation, imposing my will on others, racism, disobedience, independence, critical spirits, arrogance, vain and judgmental attitudes.

I forgive everyone that has knowingly or unknowingly contributed to my hurt.

Rejection & Lying Spirits

I renounce and forsake spirits of rejection and abandonment, all lying spirits and command them to leave me at once.

I repent for sins of judging or rejecting others, withholding love, acceptance or forgiveness.

I renounce and forsake spirits of self-hatred, self-rejection, unloving spirits, guilt, unforgiveness and anger towards myself and others.

I renounce the lie that sins done to me by others were my fault.

I renounce the shame and condemnation that have come in as a result of deep wounds, embarrassment and sins that were done to me from others.

I surrender my pain and anger and I want no benefit from it anymore.

I surrender the memories of hurtful events in my life. Take it LORD, I offer it all to you right now. Help me not take it back!

I forgive those individuals, LORD. I put them in your hands.

Forgive me for not being able to separate the sin of those that have hurt me from them as human beings that have also been hurt and used by the enemy to hurt others.

Forgive me for the times when I have not honored nor shown

respect to those in authority, parents, spouses or others.

Forgive me for broken relationships, broken vows and covenants, and please help me to do whatever I am responsible for to make things right.

I ask You to heal the breach in relationship between myself, others and You.

Drugs & Addictions

I renounce and forsake all worldly addictions including drugs, alcohol, nicotine, gambling, gluttony, compulsive physical exercise, compulsive spending, sexual sins against myself and others, pornography, and sins of excess that feed the lusts of the flesh.

I renounce and forsake the spirits of lust, bondage, Pharmacia or drugs.

Pride and Leviathan

I renounce and forsake the spirit of pride and Leviathan.

Forgive me for not humbling myself or apologizing when I

should have done so.

I repent of arguing, debating, stubbornness and being unteachable.

I renounce all covenants with the spirits known as Regret and Past. Let every agreement be nullified and broken now in Jesus name.

False Gods

I renounce and forsake all false gods and masters and all evil inheritances in my generational line.

I renounce and repent, on behalf of myself and my ancestors for any covenants or agreements made with the seven African spirits known as Papa Legba, Obtala, Oya, Oshun, Chango, Ogun and Yemmaya.

I declare there is no other God except for Jesus Christ and I break any connections or agreements that have been made through candle burning, calling on the names of false gods or saints, and invoking their assistance.

Perverse Spirit

I renounce and forsake the perverse spirit and all that is connected to it.

I renounce and forsake incubus and succubus spirits, spirits of voyeurism, homosexuality, lesbianism, perversity, masturbation, pornography, bestiality and anything connected to demonic sex.

I renounce and forsake unfruitful thoughts, fantasies, all unclean and seducing spirits, and the deceiving spirits connected to the perverse spirit.

I repent of all sexual sins.

I renounce and forsake the strongman of Baal and divorce all ungodly spirits of lust, sex and witchcraft.

Please heal the fragmentation in my soul and spirit.

I renounce ungodly soul ties, those of former lovers, false authority figures, and soul ties to anyone that would keep me from moving out of my past and into the good future You have for me. Let those ties to the past be severed now, in Jesus name.

I renounce all lies and false teaching that blinds me to truth and mocks and resists God.

I renounce all ungodly symbols that connect me to false teaching, false gods, ungodly alliances and pagan symbolism.

I accept and receive no inheritance from evil sources, only that which my heavenly Father permits and allows. Let all evil inheritances be broken off of me and my family. I put them under the blood of Jesus.

Greed

I renounce and forsake the spirit of mammon, greed, and selfishness.

I renounce and forsake the divided loyalties that come with a love for money, covetousness, idolatry and envy.

I renounce bitterness and the lie that I am not blessed by the LORD.

I renounce the lie that I will be happier with more material possessions.

I renounce the lie that somehow I am rejected or unworthy because I do not have more possessions.

I renounce the sin of comparing myself with others.

Secret Societies and False Religions

I renounce and repent for any involvement with secret societies and the ungodly covenants they demand. (If you know which ones are involved in your family history, name them).

I renounce and forsake all pledges, oaths and involvement with Freemasonry, lodges, societies or crafts by my ancestors and myself.

I renounce all false marriage covenants and mock ceremonies of secret societies.

I renounce and forsake blasphemy and taking the LORD's name in vain, as well as blasphemous oaths and pledges to Satan by any other name and alliance.

I renounce and forsake all witchcraft spirits.

I renounce and forsake all practices and traditions of Santeria and Lucemi, and praying to false gods, saints and Orishas.

I renounce and forsake the Rosy Cross, the Rosicrucian's and all ungodly alliances, oaths and associations to Grand Knights.

I renounce and forsake all false gods of Egypt as well as the lust of power, prestige and position.

I renounce and forsake all secret signs and handshakes.

I renounce and forsake all false gods, false doctrines, unholy communion and abominations.

I renounce and forsake the Luciferian doctrine.

I renounce and forsake the oaths spoken to pledge loyalties to man or idol that violated the commands of God and conscience.

I renounce all false masters associated with Freemasons, Shriners, Mormonism, Paganism, the Klu Klux Klan and other lodges and secret societies.

I renounce and forsake the false god Allah and all covenants made to the Muslim religion.

I renounce and forsake all words and phrases used as secret codes and I break agreement with all curses that were once agreed to be placed upon any and all family members, including myself and future generations.

I renounce and forsake the compass point, the cable tow, the hoodwink, the ball and chain, the apron, the noose around the neck, the sword and spear, the blindfold and the mind blinding effect of those things.

I renounce and forsake all penalties associated with breaking these ungodly oaths and covenants.

I renounce and forsake all play acting and rituals depicting murder and death, and the spirit of fear associated with death as a curse.

I revoke and break the power of agreement with these ungodly servants of darkness, Satanic worship, and all associations with those in fellowship of demonic alliances.

I command the curse to be cancelled and all ungodly covenants and agreements broken and nullified both in the earthly and spiritual realm, in the name of Jesus Christ.

I ask You, Father, Son and Holy Spirit to heal and restore every area of the physical body and ailments that have been suffered as a result of the curse brought on by any involvement by anyone in my family line.

Forgive us, I pray, for committing sin and iniquity and blasphemous acts against a Holy God, ourselves and others.

Witchcraft

I renounce, forsake and divorce myself from and break any and all agreements, covenants or involvement with: all lying spirits, the occult, demonic spirits, Native American and cultural rituals and traditions involving the use of idols, witchcraft, Voodoo, the practice of Hoodoo, root workers, witch doctors, conjuring, the practice of Juju, black magic, white magic, Wicca, and the use of mediums, familiar spirits and seducing spirits.

I renounce and forsake all oaths and rituals to false gods, witchcraft covens, sorcerers, satanists or workers of iniquity.

I renounce and forsake any and all sins involving the abuse of trust, authority, power or using our influence in an ungodly manner.

I renounce and forsake sins involving magic, sorcery, practicing charms or incantations, the use of horoscopes, tarot cards, fortune telling, astral projection, psychic energy or astrology. I will burn and destroy all books, spells, incantations, rings, and other objects that connect me to ungodly occult practices, lodges, secret societies or their unholy rituals and practices.

I renounce and ask You to break all covenants and agreements made by my ancestors that sold themselves into indentured service or slavery. Let those spiritual ties to bondage and slavery be broken now in Jesus name.

Familiar Spirits of Witchcraft

In the name and authority of Jesus Christ I also bind all Loas, mediums and familiar spirits, ungodly priests, priestesses, sorcerers and wizards that are syncretized with Catholic saints, the seven African spirits known as Papa Legba, Obtala, Oya, Oshun, Chango, Ogun and Yemmaya, and any other names by which they are known.

I bind any and all inanimate objects from being used in any sort of witchcraft, voodoo, hoodoo or other form of demonic practices, the use of wanga charms and Voodoo practices. I loose all evil spirits off of individuals, objects, and evil altars.

I command them to go to the abyss that was created for them in Jesus name.

Spirits of Divination and Snakes

I renounce and forsake all spirits of divination, the spirit of Python/ Pythos, the Serpentine spirit and all that take the form of the demonic serpent.

I renounce and ask Your forgiveness, Father, for speaking things in Your name, even prophesying, that has been out of the flesh rather than the unction of the Holy Spirit. I renounce and repent for all broken covenants, unfulfilled vows and promises, betrayal and divorce.

I ask You to please disentangle me and release me from ungodly covenants, vows, and peace treaties, and all unrighteous agreements that would bring me into relationships where I am unequally yoked with things of the kingdom of darkness, evil and wrong relationships. LORD, let there be a release of every curse that has come against me or my generational line as a result of these things.

I decree a cancellation of every form of witchcraft and curse that has resulted from my involvement or that of my generational line.

I ask You, LORD Jesus, to come and deliver me and my family from all demonic spirits that have come as a result of a curse.

I ask that You deliver me and my family from every affliction, illness, disease, allergy, or physical condition that has affected us.

I ask that You restore all the years that the enemy has stolen. Let finances, health, and relationships be restored. Let peace, joy, mental health and emotional stability be restored. Let the blessings that have been held back, stolen and hidden by the enemy be released into my hands now, in Jesus name. Let all demonic attachments be severed from me and my family line, both in the heavenly places as well as in the earthly realm.

I declare that every seed that was sown by Satan in order to perpetuate a curse or cause myself or someone else in my family line to reject my heavenly Father, the LORD Jesus Christ and Holy Spirit must now shrivel and die immediately.

Jesus, I give You permission to change what You know needs to change in my life and to convict me if I resist your Holy Spirit.

Spiritual Protection

Your word says in Isaiah 54:17 that "No weapon formed against me shall prosper, and every tongue which rises up against me in judgment shall be condemned," and that this is my inheritance in the LORD.

Right now I condemn every negative word that has been spoken over myself, my family and my future in Jesus name. I lift up (insert names of family members) and I repent for, and I condemn every negative word I have spoken over myself, my family, and our future.

I repent for negative words that I have spoken over others and I declare they will not boomerang back into my life or theirs.

I break the power of those negative words that hang in the spirit like a curse. Let every word laced with death be condemned and bear no bad fruit in Jesus name.

I declare that those negative words will no longer ring in my ears, nor in those that have heard or repeated negative, condemning words.

I declare that words that have been used as a weapon will no longer ring in the ears of my loved ones and hinder their faith or their future in Jesus name. From this day forward, I declare their ears shall be deaf to condemning words and only faith shall prosper in their heart, mind and spirit in Jesus name.

Generation Issues

Father, I repent for these sins on behalf of myself and my family to the tenth generation back.

I thank You for Your forgiveness and cleansing of these sins.

I declare that when I am tested, the Spirit of God will arise within me and bring me into a place of victory. I give You permission in advance of any situation I may encounter that You and Your Holy Spirit may change my actions, words and responses so that I honor You. Please reign and rule over my emotions.

Enemy, according to the scripture in James 4:7, as I am now submitted to God, you must flee from me.

I command you to take everything that you have put on me, everything that you have tormented me with, every sickness and GO!

I command you to pay restitution at no less than a 7-fold return, according to Proverbs 6:31 in every place that you have brought poverty, defeat, robbery, or death and destruction.

Father God, I ask that You cleanse my mind of all unfruitful thoughts, fantasies, and works of the flesh.

I thank You for the blood that Jesus Christ has shed on my behalf, and I appropriate the power of His blood and the resurrection power of Your Holy Spirit to every sin, transgression and generational iniquity over myself and my family line.

By the power and authority of the blood of Jesus Christ, I declare my victory.

Satan, you no longer have authority to torment me or my children with iniquitous sin patterns. Your plan is cut off now in Jesus name. God has promised in Hebrews 8:12 that He will be merciful to our unrighteousness and our sins and lawless deeds He will remember no more.

Release the Blessings

I loose myself and my family from demonic attachments that have been invoked for safety, protection, healing, provision, prophecy, and financial blessing.

I declare the names of God over every name in heaven, in the earth and under the earth.

I declare the name El Shaddai over me and my family, for He is the God that is mighty and He is our sustainer.

I declare the name El Elyon over us, for He is exalted as the MOST HIGH GOD. He is exalted as the Sovereign One.

I declare Jehovah Nissi over me and my family, for He is the one that causes victory over our enemies.

I declare Jehovah Saboath over us, for He is the LORD of Hosts of angelic armies.

I declare the name Jehovah Rapha over myself and my household for He is the One that heals.

I declare Jehovah Jireh over me and my family, for He is the one that provides.

I declare the name of El Gmulot, for He is the God of recompense and the one who spoils the plans of the enemy.

I declare the name of Jehovah Mekeddishkem over me and my family for He is our sanctifier.

I declare the name of Jehovah Elohim over myself and my household, for it is He is strong and causes men to fear the LORD.

I declare the name of Jehovah Adon over this land, for He is Master, Owner, LORD and covenant keeping God.

I declare the name of Jehovah Roi over us, for the LORD is our Shepherd, protector and keeper.

I declare the name of Jehovah Shammah, for the LORD is present.

I declare the name of Jehovah Tdiskenu over myself and my family for He is our righteousness.

I declare the name of Jehovah Shalom over us, for He is our peace.

I release the Spirit of Adoption over myself and my family members, to draw others into personal relationship with the LORD Jesus Christ and to shed abroad the revelation of Abba Father in the hearts of every individual, in Jesus name.

Declaration of Faith

Jesus, You are the Son of God, and You are seated victoriously at the right hand of the Father.

Today I declare that the enemy is defeated where I am concerned.

You are my Master, my LORD and my Savior. Please come with Your Holy Spirit and heal my mind, my emotions, my thoughts, my confession and my memories.

I forgive those who failed to reach out to me when I was hurting.

I forgive those who have intentionally caused hurt and pain to me and my family, and those that have done it unintentionally.

I ask You to bless, heal and deliver those that have acted in ways that have hurt me or caused harm to me or my family.

I will trust You to judge fairly and mete out any justice in these issues.

Bless those that have hurt me, lied about me, or deliberately caused harm to me or my family, and set me free from offense. I release them to you now.

Please forgive me Father, Jesus, and Holy Spirit for willingly disregarding Your words and Your Spirit when You have tried to get through to me.

Please heal my trust issues with you and others.

Please heal the issues related to my past, my present and my future.

Heal my hope, my faith and my love.

Heal any areas of grief, heaviness, unbelief, and let the renewed mind of Christ be strengthened and formed in me each and every day.

Thank You for releasing into me a spirit of Faith, a spirit of Obedience, the spirit of Adoption, the spirit of Revelation and Truth.

Now tell me LORD, what I need to do as an act of faith that will release my breakthrough.

Confirm it and convict me that I will not neglect to do whatever You tell me to do. Thank You for eternal life, health, and victory, and for restoring my life and my future, in Jesus' precious name, Amen.

CONFESSING THE SINS OF OUR NATION'S FOREFATHERS AND HEALING FOR NATIVE AMERICANS

Father God, Lord Jesus and Holy Spirit:

I come to You on behalf of myself and all those in my ancestral line that came before me. I ask for Your forgiveness for our sins, and today I acknowledge that many of us sinned by never asking for Jesus Christ to be our Lord and Savior. Many of us committed sins and trespasses in rebellion to Your ways. Please hear my prayer and let the blood of Jesus cleanse my ancestral line from all unrighteousness. I take You as My Lord, and ask that You adopt me as Your child. You paid for me with Your blood, Lord Jesus, and I thank You that You went to the cross in my place.

Father, I also come to you as a citizen of the United States, and I ask You to forgive the sins of our forefathers. I ask You to forgive the sins of those that pioneered and settled this land, and the pagan practices, cultures and traditions brought in from foreign lands. Forgive, I pray, our presidential and political leaders that broke treaties and treacherously removed the boundary lines of Native Americans and others to claim them as their own. For it is written:

"Don't cheat your neighbor by moving the ancient boundary markers set up by previous generations." Prov. 22:28

Forgive us for encroaching on property that didn't belong to us and cheating rightful heirs out of their inheritance, for it is also written, "Do not move an ancient boundary stone or encroach on the fields of the fatherless," in Proverbs 23:10.

Forgive us for impoverishing Native American families, forcing them out of their homes, for making slaves of other races and nationalities; for causing others to feel overcome with jealousy, fear, anger and desire vengeance against those who treated them wrongfully.

Forgive us for the grief we caused, the injustices and the bloodshed.

Forgive us for broken covenants, vows and agreements and for the curses that came as a result of those actions. Although I may not have personally taken part in these sins, I understand that there is a need to recognize the sins of those that came before us and I ask for the blood of Jesus to atone for these things so that this land can be cleansed.

Please allow all those that have been affected by this

generational root of bitterness, grief and poverty now find the grace to forgive the generations of mistreatment and injustices. I choose to forgive anyone that I have been offended with. I choose to forgive those that I feel are responsible for my pain or bitterness.

Father, I renounce all false gods and masters. According to Your word, O God, in Deuteronomy 7:5, You commanded Your people to destroy ungodly altars and break down their sacred pillars. Let these prayers of renouncement accomplish the destruction of all ungodly altars in my family, in my generational line, and in this nation.

On behalf of myself, my generational line, the founding fathers of this nation and all political leaders in this land, I identify with these sins and the need to acknowledge them to You so that our land may be healed.

Therefore, I renounce the demonic spirits of Hoodoo, Voodoo, Satanism, and all spirits of witchcraft and magic in the name of Jesus Christ. I renounce all practices and demonic spirits associated with black magic, the Cherokee, Chickasaw, the Creek, Seminole, Choctaw, the Blackfoot, Cree, Crow, Pauite, Shoebone, Cheyenne, Sioux, the Ute, Pawnee, the Navajo, Shawnee and Apache customs and traditions.

I renounce African religions, the Catholic religion and their saints, patrons and patronesses; familiar spirit guides and any and all other false gods and deities of various religions.

I renounce the use of tobacco for ceremonial or ungodly religious purposes and any and all power associated with it to be rendered impotent, paralyzed and powerless, according to what You have already done on the cross, Lord Jesus.

I renounce all familiar spirits that may be associated with Native American dances that involve the use of conjuring demons, the use demonic power, psychic energy, ancient witchcraft practices, sorcery, charms, spells, incantations and magic. Let all ungodly altars be silent and dismantled now.

Let the blood of Jesus cover those individuals that have participated in demonic worship whether or not they participated knowingly or unknowingly. I ask You to deliver them and set them free from all deception, Lord Jesus. Let Your Holy Spirit reveal the truth that will free people from demonic oppression, possession, and deception. Let the blinders fall off. Give them a spirit of revelation and an understanding heart that they might come to know the One and True Living God, Jesus Christ.

I renounce all customs of speaking word curses on their

enemies through traditional songs. Forgive us for things we did and practices that were accepted that had a spirit of death and cursing bound to the words that were spoken. Let all word curses be broken now in the spiritual and earthly realms. Let those words laced with death lose all power and cease to ring in the ears of those who have heard them. I bind the spirit of death that is associated with these customs and culture and forbid the spirits of death and hell from being released. I command them to go back now to the place where Jesus sends them and forever be bound into captivity. I declare that the spirits of death and hell will no longer advance in the name and authority of Jesus Christ.

On behalf of myself, my ancestors and the forefathers of this nation, I renounce demonic attachments associated with gambling and ceremonial gambling. I loose the demonic spirits and spiritual enforcers off of all objects used in gambling and command them to return to the abyss created for all demons.

Let the spirits of lust, greed, selfishness and bondage be bound in the name and authority of Jesus Christ. I pray, O God, let the Spirit of Liberty be released to free all people that have been bound by sin and addiction. Let them be loosed from their bondage in Jesus name.

Let all demons be loosed off of individuals, out of homes,

offices, businesses, churches, and expelled out of the land that You have given to Your rightful heirs. I ask You, Lord Jesus, to grant an order for eviction from the court of heaven that commands all encroachers, squatters, soothsayers, and those who practice demonic witchcraft off of the land. I command these demonic spirits to be sent back to the place prepared for all demons where they must be bound and confined until the day of their eternal judgment in the lake of fire.

I thank You, Lord Jesus, Heavenly Father and Holy Spirit for releasing Your power against the works of evil, that it might come to a quick and sudden end. I ask that You also release the power of Your Holy Spirit to bring forth forgiveness, compassion, grace and healing. Let there be signs, wonders and miracles, to the glory of the Son of God, Jesus Christ.

I ask that You display Your power against the works of darkness, evil and Satan, that the workers of sorcery, demonic magic, witchcraft, spells, incantations, and every form of demonic power would be seen as inferior to that of Your Holy Spirit . I ask that the name of Jesus would be glorified and the enemy be put to an open shame.

I ask that everything the enemy has done to conspire, entrap, ensnare, falsely accuse, gain a false judgment by deceit, bribery or falsehood be overturned.

Let all who oppress Your children and hinder them from their divine purpose and assignments be stopped and brought to justice. Let righteous judgment prevail. I ask that You would, according to this petition, grant victory and justice for those that have waited for Your intervention.

Please let Your restoration be upon us all. I pray for the blessings that have been blocked up, barricaded, unlawfully stolen, hidden or plundered - and I tell them, *"Come back into your rightful generational line. Come back into those families and let the blessings flow abundantly in Jesus name."*

Let the power of Christ be displayed, the name of Jesus glorified, as You destroy the works of the evil one. In Jesus name, Amen.

This prayer is written specifically for African-Americans but can by prayed by anyone that may be unsure of their ancestry, or has reason to believe that the things mentioned in this prayer could be applicable to their life and family. When it comes to deliverance, it pays to be thorough.

PRAYER TO HEAL AFRICAN-AMERICAN HERITAGE AND CLEANSE BLOODLINE CURSES

Dear Heavenly Father,

I seek Your help, the help that is only available to me through Jesus Christ, the blood of the lamb, and His Holy Spirit. I desperately want to be cleansed from demonic spirits, unbroken curses and familiar spirits that have been a part of my life, through my family members, from even before my birth. I ask You, Jesus Christ, Lord of all, to be my Lord and Savior. I ask You to cleanse me from all unrighteousness and set me free.

I repent for any way that I have knowingly or unknowingly given place to demonic spirits and allowed them to access my life. I renounce the sins of my parents, grandparents, and other ancestors; this day I divorce the enemy, Satan, and all other false gods and religions.

I renounce fear, self-will, lust, control and confusion. I break every ungodly covenant, oath and vow that may have been spoken by myself or any of my ancestors, knowing that this is forbidden by Your word. Lord Jesus, please let me be released from any ungodly alliances, covenants, or legally binding treaties that were enacted between me, my family, and demonic spirits.

I renounce and divorce the enemy, Satan, and any evil spirit that may have been called into my life. I renounce the spirits of Santeria, Lucumi, African gods and all familiar spirits associated with rituals, prayers, customs and traditions. I renounce the seven African spirits known as Papa Legba, Obtala, Oya, Oshun, Chango, Ogun and Yemmaya, in the name of Jesus Christ.

I renounce all Loas, mediums and familiar spirits, ungodly priests, priestesses, sorcerers and wizards.

I renounce African and cultural witchcraft, Yoruba traditions, shamans, witch doctors, their rituals and voodoo that have been practiced by my ancestors. I want nothing to do with those practices, rituals, and traditions and I renounce them all, in Jesus name.

I renounce divination and conjuring of all familiar spirits of the dead and those that my ancestors and family members have participated in. I renounce all soul ties to familiar and familial protectors, spirit guides, scribes and messengers, diviners and ungodly priests, false fathers and mothers, and those known as Babalawo.

I renounce all inanimate objects used for divining purposes, including casting of chains. Lord Jesus, I ask that You break every ungodly chain that has tied me to these things that I am now renouncing.

I renounce all animal and material sacrifices made on my behalf or those in my family line. I renounce all human involvement for the sake of divining information, the use of familiar spirits, spirit guides, and false gods. I renounce all blood that was shed from any source that was tied to my life through the use of occult practices. I renounce all herbalists and root workers that concocted medicines, potions, magic and incantations used in Ayajo.

I repent and renounce any participation of myself or those in my family line in the indoctrination, apprenticeship, spiritual journey, rituals or rites of passage of myself or others into occult practices.

I renounce all lying, devious, deceptive and manipulative spirits that were inherited as a curse.

I renounce the spirits of fear, suspicion, rejection, loneliness, inferiority, insecurity, poverty, death and hell that have come into my life. I renounce the spirit of abandonment, unloving spirits, guilt and condemnation. Lord Jesus, fill me with Your peace and love.

I lift up myself to You right now. I pray that You would help me embrace whatever traumatic or negative memories that I have either blocked out or forgotten, if recalling those memories can be used to release healing.

I repent for any sin or involvement of myself and my ancestors that opened doors to the occult through witchcraft and occult magic. I renounce Voodoo, the practices of making and wearing charms, amulets and making Ouanga. I renounce the works of evil associated with the bitter roots of the evil tree known as the *figuier maudit,* and any Ouangas made to practice witchcraft over others.

I renounce all soul ties, familiar spirits and bondages associated with Voodoo Kings, Queens, priests and priestesses. I renounce any and all covenants that were made with spirits of darkness and Satan himself. I hereby divorce the enemy and cancel any contracts that were made knowingly or unknowingly by myself or any of my ancestors.

I renounce and forsake any and all customs, traditions, practices and beliefs that are forbidden by God, that originated with West Africans, the French, Spanish, Creole and Caribbean people.

I renounce and break any soul ties now to the bondages, mindset, beliefs and emotional pain and bitterness that came through slavery, as a result of injustice, fear and oppression.

I renounce and break all associations with idolatry, familiar spirits, witchcraft and rebellion that originated with the Fon people and other groups known as the Bambara, Mandinga, Wolof, Ewe, Fulb, Narde, Minajjhhhjjii, Dahomean, Yoruba, Chamba, Congo, Ibo, Ado, Hausa, and Sango cultural practices.

I renounce all associations with the Haitian Maroon rebellion and massacre of other people. I renounce and divorce myself from all spirits of war.

I renounce the kinship, soul ties and solidarity of former slaves that has held anyone in my family in bondage. I renounce and break all covenants with the spirits known as Regret, Past, Bitterness, Jealousy and the Perverse spirit.

I renounce the false God Allah associated with the Muslim religion.

I renounce all mixture and perversity that came from Catholic traditions and religious practices, ancestor worship and African, Caribbean or Creole culture.

I ask You, Holy Spirit, to show me anything else that is

significant to my life or family. I give You permission to dislodge memories that are stuck. I pray that You highlight any specific memories or situations, objects or possessions that are related to anything that is connected to a curse.

I pray that You would supernaturally remove the hurtful memories and the trauma of past events out of my mind, emotions, memories and out of my physical body. I ask that You would lift all remnants of painful events and the trauma that was created as a result of that pain. Lift it all out of the very cells of my body.

Let my ears not remember hurtful words spoken to me, about me, by me, or by others. Let my heart release all unforgiveness, anger, fear, rejection, pain and shame. I speak now and declare complete healing and freedom from every painful event in my life.

I declare that painful memories and hurtful words will not circulate in my mind and emotions any longer in the name and authority of Jesus Christ. I pray that no cell in my body would retain unforgiveness, bitterness, anger, hatred, fear, condemnation, regret, rejection or self-hatred. I pray that my physical body would no longer be in agreement with any negative emotions in Jesus name.

I release myself and others from the pain of their past, and the poor decisions they made as a result of their brokenness. I release them from guilt, shame, regret and bitterness now, in Jesus name. I forgive and release those who willfully and spitefully inflicted pain and suffering on me and my family.

I forgive and release those who had wicked intentions and gave themselves over to evil, in order to afflict, torment, and delight themselves in causing me or my family members pain. I give them over to You, Father, to do with as You choose; knowing that You are a just God and vengeance belongs to You. I choose to trust You in matters concerning justice and judgement towards others, knowing that as a matter of my will, I choose to forgive and am therefore free in Christ.

Let me remember only the good about those the enemy used to cause pain. I pray that my heart and mind would agree that I am in an entirely new day and I am able to graciously forgive those that treated me wrong. I forgive anyone that caused insult, offense, or physical injury to me, my family and those from my past. I take authority over the past and apply the blood of Jesus to every door the enemy has used to exploit pain, injury and injustice. I declare these doors are now closed and the enemy can no longer use them in Jesus name.

I ask Your forgiveness for any doors that I have accidentally opened to the enemy through trying to comfort myself with artificial means. I renounce and break every unintentional agreement that I may have made with spirits of fear, lust, anger, greed, gluttony, anger, bitterness, unforgiveness, unloving spirits, idolatry or a perverse spirit that also inflicts wounds on others. I submit to You, Holy Spirit, and command all ungodly spirits to leave me now, in the name and authority of Jesus Christ. I command all unclean spirits to go back to where they came from. I appropriate the blood of Christ over every part of my life, and others for whom I pray.

Let every weight be released. Let every hindrance be released. Let all that does not originate from the kingdom of heaven be released out of my mind, body, emotions and memories. Every weakness be filled now with wholeness and perfect soundness in the name and authority of Jesus Christ. Holy Spirit, fill me now with Your fullness, strength and power in Jesus name. Fill me with joy, peace, and a release of supernatural healing that radiates from the inside out. I declare that by Your stripes I have been healed, according to Is. 53:5. Thank you for the blood You shed, Lord Jesus, that makes healing a reality. I thank You for revival, restoration, healing and complete regeneration in Jesus name.

PRAYER TO DISMANTLE EVIL ALTARS

Father,

In the name and authority of the Lord Jesus Christ, I hereby release a decree against all ungodly altars and evil thrones.

Whereas, the enemy, hereafter known as Satan and all those under his influence, has conspired to perpetuate a curse against the people in this city and geographic region, including me and my family;

Whereas, the enemy has refused to leave me and my family alone, but has continually harassed, tormented, afflicted, robbed, deceived, murdered, accused, divided and destroyed;

Whereas, Satan and demonic spirits has made corporate covenants with evil minded people and spiritual forces in order to terminate the life and spirit of Your people;

Whereas, the enemy has plotted to tempt Your people to greed, rebellion and idolatry so that they would sin against You, thereby hindering You from drawing close to Your people;

Whereas, the enemy has contracted with services from unholy priests and unrighteous ministers in order to invoke curses upon Your people, to weaken them and make them susceptible to failure and defeat;

Whereas, the enemy and adversary has strategized how to deceive Your people through divination and fraud;

Whereas, the enemy has made strategies to bring division, discord and disunity in families, churches, ministries and throughout this geographic region so as to cut off a move of Your Spirit;

Whereas, the enemy has exalted himself as a God and erected altars to himself, thereby depriving You of worship;

Whereas, these ungodly altars include abortion clinics, where the blood of innocent lives are shed, thereby further empowering Satan and demonic forces to carry out evil plans;

Whereas, these ungodly and evil altars are for the sole purpose of perpetuating torment and affliction upon Your people and those in this geographic region;

Whereas, ancient covenants and ancestral traditions have empowered the enemy to continue to enact curses upon Your people so that they are carried away with grief, torment of soul and unbelief towards You;

Whereas these ungodly covenants have handed our families, the citizens of our cities and this geographic region over to bondage, making the citizens thereof serve ungodly kings and rulers, and have made people slaves to demonic spiritual powers;

Whereas, the result of these actions by the enemy and his followers produces captivity, slavery to sin and judgment from God;

Therefore, I ask that as the Just Judge of Heaven and Earth, You charge the enemy with the aforementioned crimes against humanity. I request that he be brought up on charges, chained, and brought to the court of heaven. I petition the court in a class action suit against the evil one known as Satan, the Father of Lies, the Deceiver, the Thief, the Accuser of the Brethren, Diablo, the one who Divides, the Murderer, and any and all names by which he is otherwise known. Let all evil princes, warlords, witches, wizards, satanic priests and those practicing demonic sorcery also be named as defendants.

In Your law, Father, it is written in Deuteronomy 12:2-4, "You shall utterly destroy all the places where the nations whom you shall dispossess serve their gods, on the high mountains and on the hills and under every green tree. "You shall tear down their altars and smash their sacred pillars and burn their Asherim and you shall cut down the engraved images of their gods and obliterate their name from that place. "You shall not act like this toward the LORD your God."

It is also written in Deuteronomy 7:5, Exodus 34:14, Leviticus 26:30 and Numbers 33:52 that we, Your people, are to tear down ungodly altars and destroy the high places where evil thrones rule.

Again, in Exodus 23:24 it is written: "Do not bow down before their gods or worship them or follow their practices. You must demolish them and break their sacred stones to pieces."

Therefore, let all evil altars be silenced. Let the spirit of python, witchcraft, familiar spirits and divination be silenced and sent back to the abyss created for them in the name and authority of the Lord Jesus Christ.

Let all those that practice witchcraft and sorcery against others lose all power and effectiveness to carry out their plans, in Jesus name.

Let the enemy and all adversaries be set upon themselves in

confusion, so that they cannot communicate, form plans or strategize, in Jesus name, according to Genesis 11:7-9, 1 Samuel 14:20 and Judges 7:22.

Let praise and worship arise to Jesus Christ that sets ambushes and routes the enemy, for it is written in 2 Chron. 20:20 that when Your people began to praise You, You set ambushes for their enemies which caused the enemy to turn upon himself. Let the enemies of God be completely defeated in Jesus name.

Let all sacrifices to false gods cease immediately in Jesus name, for Your law states that man shall have no other gods before You, as it is written in 2 Chronicles 20: 3. I also request in the name of Jesus Christ that all abortion clinics where human sacrifices are made and all altars where the blood of innocents is shed must close down immediately, for these act as evil altars where the enemy gains power.

Let Your fire be kindled upon the foundations of evil mountains and burn into the lowest hell according to Deuteronomy 32:22.

Let the foundations of evil altars hear Your shout, O God! Let their walls be torn down and her towers fall according to Jeremiah 50:15.

Let the sword of the Lord be released against evil foundations and altars where satan is worshiped, according to Jeremiah 46:10.

Let evil foundations and demonic altars be shaken according to Acts. 16:26.

Let Your hand be stretched out against the destroying mountains that destroy the earth according to Jeremiah 51:25.

Let the foundations of Egypt be torn down, according to Ezekiel 30:4, and let the wealth of the wicked be transferred into the hands of the righteous, according to Prov. 13:22.

Let all those that are involved in making sacrifices to false gods, satanic worship and involved in demonic sorcery immediately become disillusioned and disappointed in their false gods, reject and renounce all covenants, contracts and loyalty to evil spirits. Let them burn their magic books and come over to the Lord's side, as it is written in Acts 19:17-19. "Many of those who had believed kept coming, confessing and disclosing their practices. And many of those who practiced magic brought their books together and burned them in the sight of everyone…"

Let the word of God grow mightily and prevail, according to Acts 19:20.

Let those who have been poisoned by bitterness and bound by iniquity repent and be saved according to Acts 8:13 and vs. 22-24.

Let every intended curse that the enemy wants to put upon Your people be turned into a blessing, in Jesus name, according to Deuteronomy 23:5.

Let every form of deception, fraud and intent to injure your people be unraveled and come to nothing, in Jesus name, for it is written that no weapon formed against us shall prosper according to Is. 54:17.

Let angels be released to tear down evil altars and unseat ungodly rulers, according to Ephesians 2:6, for I am seated with Christ in heavenly places above principalities and powers in high places.

Let principalities and powers be spoiled, according to Jeremiah 51:56 and Col. 2:16. Let the God of recompense, El Gmulot, destroy the works of evil in Jesus name.

Let God arise and Your enemies be scattered according to Psalm 68:1,2.

Let the covenants and ancient traditions of the enemy be halted now, in Jesus name. Let people return to making covenants with God their Father according to Exodus 24:7-8.

Let the fire of God consume the divination of the enemy according to 1 Kings 18:40, and let all ungodly altars be silenced and void of power.

Let altars to God Our Father be constructed in our homes, workplaces and throughout the land, giving glory to the Lord Jesus Christ.

It is also written in Proverbs 6:31 that when the thief is caught he must repay with a seven-fold return and may have to give up all the substance of his house. I petition the court for the full amount due, and ask that You make the thief give up his entire house full of goods.

You also stated in Proverbs 13:22 in the word of God that the wealth of the wicked is stored up for the righteous. I petition the court for compensation of the losses of previous years and that You would grant my request. I ask that the enemy must repay retroactive compensation for past losses, due and payable immediately by the amount set by the court.

Let it be known that it is also written that we are not slaves, but sons, daughters and heirs. For Jesus Christ, our Liberator, bought our freedom when he was crucified and resurrected on our behalf. I ask that the thief must be declared guilty and a favorable judgment towards Your people would be granted. I also ask for angels to be put on assignment to administer the distribution of wealth, blessings, healings, miracles, breakthrough, restoration and oversee that justice is brought to Your people.

I ask that all false judgments against Your people be overturned, and that Your people who have been falsely accused, slandered and shamed due to the evil plots of the enemy would be vindicated.

As a blood bought child of God, I petition the court to consider the charges brought against the defendant(s) and I call the LORD JESUS CHRIST to act as our defending counsel. I also petition the witness of HOLY SPIRIT to declare the truth in accordance to the aforementioned charges.

Please let it be recognized by the court that this appeal is not based on any righteousness or good deeds on behalf of the plaintiffs. In fact, we respectfully acknowledge that we have no personal merit by which we may stand before the court. Your Honor, the plaintiffs should be acquitted of any counter charges brought by the enemy, based on the shed blood of Jesus Christ. I approach the court because it is written in Hebrews 4:16 that I may come boldly to the throne of grace to find help and mercy in the time of my need. I acknowledge that as plaintiffs, we are merely sinners that have been saved by Your grace, and we ask that You give consideration to the fact that the blood of the Lord Jesus Christ, our brother and Your Son, paid our debt in full with His very life. His sacrifice is not in vain.

Therefore, I request that any and all excuses or arguments made by the defendant(s) shall be upheld as an objection, rendered null and void, and be stricken from the court records. I also ask that Your people are granted the eviction notice that is immediately served upon the enemy which forces him out of my home, family, and the land in this geographic region. Let Your angels chain the enemy and render all adversaries paralyzed, silenced and impotent of all power. Thank You for hearing my petition and for granting my request . In Jesus name, Amen.

The following prayer is written for San Diego County, but you may use it as an example for your own city. Just substitute the name of your city, state and county in the appropriate places.

A PRAYER AND DECREE FOR CITY TRANSFORMATION

May the peace of God dwell in this city and may His dominion reign over all of _____ County. Let the foundation of this city be built upon righteousness, truth, mercy and justice. May the Lord look with favor upon us, and His blessing be poured out in every household. May the abundance of the Father's love and goodness release restoration; and let there be healing to every household and family. May this land be restored and our economy prosperous. Let every family be blessed with more than enough and a generous spirit to be a blessing to others, in Jesus name. Amen.

In the name and authority of Jesus Christ I decree:

An end to confusion, strife, and disorder. I call all things into Divine order and subject to the Lordship of Jesus Christ.

Let there be a release of the fear of the Lord, light and truth over (*enter name of your city*) according to Genesis 1:3 and John 16:13.

I decree an end to human trafficking, prostitution, rape, theft, murder and all violence. I declare the walls of this city "Salvation" and our gates, "Praise," according to Isaiah 60:18.

Let the Love of God be poured out through His Holy Spirit, so that people have an encounter with their Heavenly Father, and know that they are valued, esteemed and loved by Him.

I declare the economic conditions and commerce of our city are healed. I declare there shall be no lack of good paying jobs, affordable housing and provision for the necessities of life, according to Psalm 23:1.

I declare wisdom and godly counsel shall come forth from our government leaders. I bless them to receive divine strategies and inspired ideas; to get around the obstacles that will enable them to govern the people with righteousness, equity and justice in Jesus name.

I bless our military personnel, police, border patrol, firemen, paramedics and all first responders with safety and protection. I ask You to release angels to be dispatched that will carry messages of wisdom and to oversee, guide, protect and preserve life.

I declare blessing over honest, reputable businesses. I speak prosperity over them in the name of Jesus our Lord.

I declare dishonest, disreputable businesses and those that are shell companies for immoral and illegal activity shall dry up, in the name and authority of Jesus Christ.

I declare an end to abandoned, abused and neglected children. I declare every child to have the safety, love and protection of a loving family.

I declare an end to hopelessness and homelessness in Jesus name. I speak new opportunities and restoration to those that have suffered great loss and hardship.

I declare freedom from addictions, mental illness, bondage and brokenness, in the name and authority of Jesus Christ.

I declare supernatural healing to be released in Jesus name.

I declare blessing and increase, raises and promotions, retroactive compensation, recovery of losses, divine connections, favor and restoration over every individual in _____ County.

I declare the enemy shall have no right of remembrance in our city and throughout _____County. I declare Jesus is Lord over

_____ County and throughout the State of _____. I declare the name of Jesus Christ over every other name according to Philippians 2:9-11 and Romans 14:11.

I decree an open heaven over _____ County. I release revelation and truth to set the captives free according to John 8:32.

I declare this is the gate of the Lord, the gate of righteousness according to Psalm 118:20.

I declare that Jesus Christ has reconciled all things unto Himself and His peace dwells in this city, according to Colossians 1:20.

I decree a release of the Spirit of Divine Love, Forgiveness, Humility, Grace and Repentance over this county and throughout this city according to John 3:16,17.

I decree angelic assistance and intervention is released to dismantle demonic thrones, ungodly rulers, principalities and powers, and ungodly authority structures.

I decree all demonic spirits are bound in the name and authority of Jesus Christ and we render them paralyzed, impotent and powerless, sent back to the abyss now.

I decree a supernatural release of miracles, signs and wonders by the work of the Holy Spirit, according to Mark 16:17,18.

I decree a release of creative solutions for entrepreneurs and strategies for businesses to prosper to come forth, according to Proverbs 8:12.

I decree a release of supernatural wisdom and understanding to provide insight and foresight to God's people.

I decree a release of the Spirit of Adoption, and regeneration and renewal in the minds and hearts of the citizens of this county. People will walk in the identity as sons and daughters of the Most High God, according to Romans 8:15.

I decree a release of the breath of God to bring revival, renewal, restoration and transformation, according to Ezek. 36:33-35.

I declare these things in the name and authority of Jesus Christ, and we thank You, Father, that as we do, You cause them to be established so that light will shine upon our ways. Amen.

DECREE TO ENFORCE GOD'S DOMINION IN YOUR CITY

Abba Father,

I come before you today to give you thanks, to recognize You and You alone as Supreme Authority. I declare Jesus is Lord, over my life, over my city, and this nation; and specifically over this geographic region.

Lord Jesus, Your words in Mark 3:27 remind me that I must bind the strongman before his house can be divided and his goods taken away. I declare Jesus is King of Kings and Lord of Lords, the MOST HIGH GOD, and I declare your name above every other name. I command every knee to bow to the name of Jesus Christ our Lord, and I ask You to release your warring angels to bind the strongmen of Idolatry, Witchcraft - specifically Voodoo, Rebellion and the Perverse spirit.

I ask You to bind the strongmen known as Appolyan, Leviathan, and the spirit of Whoredoms in the name and authority of Jesus Christ.

I ask that You send Your angels to bind up the strongmen known as Heaviness, Abandonment, Bondage and Infirmity.

I ask You to bind up the spirit of Death and Hell, Insanity and Mental Illness, Rejection, Anger, War and Fear – let each of these strongmen be bound, silenced and sent back to the abyss that was created for them, held for the time of their everlasting judgment.

In the name and authority of the Lord Jesus Christ, I now loose:

The Spirit of Humility, The Spirit of Grace and Repentance, The Spirit of Adoption, the Spirit of Liberty, Purity, the Spirit of Might, The Spirit of Understanding, the Spirit of Righteousness, The Love of God, The Fear of the Lord, The Spirit of Peace, The Joy of the Lord, The Spirit of Truth, and the Spirit of Resurrection Life.

Let the gifts of Your Holy Spirit be activated and released to bring healing to this land, in Jesus name.

I declare that according to what You have done on the cross and through my prophetic declarations that these demonic spirits are bound in the name and authority of Jesus Christ. Let Your hand break the power of ungodly altars for in Deut. 12:31 it is written, "You must not worship the Lord your God the way these other nations worship their gods, they do all kinds of detestable things the Lord hates." According to the work of the cross of Christ and His resurrection, I command these ungodly spirits to be rendered powerless, impotent, paralyzed and silent.

In the name and authority of Jesus Christ I also bind all mediums and familiar spirits, ungodly priests, priestesses, sorcerers and wizards and any other names which they may be called. I bind any and all inanimate objects from being used in any sort of witchcraft, voodoo, hoodoo or other form of demonic practices and loose all evil spirits off of individuals, objects, and evil altars. I command them to go to the abyss that was created for them in Jesus name, for it is written in 1 Corinthians 10:14 that we are to flee from idolatry, and again in 1 Cor. 10:20 we are commanded not to be participants with demons.

I release the curse upon all false doctrine and doctrine of devils, and we declare, in the name and authority of Jesus Christ, that the perverse root that brings error must dry up and die immediately. I declare the perverse root from perverse trees to be cut off from this land and to bear no more fruit, for it is written in Matthew 7:15-20 that bad trees cannot bear good fruit. Let every demonic tree be cut down and thrown into the fire. I declare that evil and perversity will not prosper in Jesus name. Let good trees with their roots in the Lord Jesus Christ be planted in every place where evil once prospered.

I ask You to plant the torch of the Lord in places that have been darkened by sin. Let Your ministers arise as flames of fire, passion and demonstrate the power of Your kingdom.

In the name and authority of Jesus Christ, I bind the spirit of Chaos. I release Divine Order and call all things into alignment now, saying, *"Let there be order,"* in Jesus name. I call for unity, healing, restoration, and the glory of the Lord to be released in every home and over this city and region, in Jesus name.

I loose every person from demonic attachments and influences pertaining to false spiritual fathers and mothers. I declare deaf ears are now opened to hear what the Spirit of the Lord is communicating according to Isaiah 35:5 and Isaiah 29:18,19.

I loose every person from demonic attachments and influences pertaining to mind control, emotions, mental illness, depression and insanity. I declare healing, clarity and restoration of sight to those that have been blinded according to Psalm 147:3, Isaiah 42:7 and Isaiah 32:3.

I loose every person from demonic attachments and the curse that brings sickness, disease and infirmity. I declare supernatural healing, restoration and the release of the gifts of Holy Spirit to heal and deliver according to Mark 16:18 and Matthew 11:5.

I loose every person from spirits of poverty, death and hell.

I loose honest and reputable businesses from demonic attachments that impoverish, steal and destroy their ability to prosper. I declare the promise in 3 John 1: 2 that as their souls prosper, they will also enjoy prosperity in every part of their lives, and businesses will prosper.

I declare restoration, increase and blessing. I declare raises and promotions, creative and witty ideas, and retroactive compensation to be released. According to Proverbs 6:31 the thief has been caught. He must restore with a 7 fold increase and give up the entire substance of his house. I declare the losses of previous years to be restored to those whose right it is, according to 2 Kings 8:6.

I loose every person from the perverse spirit. I loose individuals from unclean spirits of lust, and all things that are perverse and ungodly.

I declare a release of Holy Spirit to bring forth conviction, humility, repentance and a desire for purity in every person in this land.

I declare that unholy things will not satisfy and will no longer be desired or sought after. I declare a release of passion and hunger for the Lord to prevail in the hearts and minds of those in this geographic region.

I declare that according to Colossians 1:13 people are delivered from the domain of darkness and transferred into the kingdom of God's dear Son, Jesus Christ., and those that hunger shall be filled according to Matthew 5:6.

I loose every person from demonic warring spirits: fear, anger, accusation, jealousy, slander, envy, strife, unforgiveness and bitterness.

I release the curse to dry up and cut off the roots of war, bitterness, the perverse spirit, rebellion and idolatry in this land.

I declare a release of heavenly wisdom from Holy Spirit; unity, forgiveness and mercy in Jesus name.

I declare a release of the light of Christ and the spirit of humility, grace and forgiveness to wash over the hearts and minds of every individual in this land according to 1 John 2:8-10.

I declare that people will abide in the light of Jesus Christ and will come into unity now, the unity that releases a great anointing and the glory of God, according to Psalm 133.

I loose every person from demonic attachments that have been invoked for safety, protection, healing, provision, prophecy, and financial blessing.

I declare the names of God over every name in heaven, in the earth and under the earth. I declare the name El Shaddai over this land, for You are the God that is mighty and You are our sustainer.

I declare the name El Elyon over this land, for You are exalted as the MOST HIGH GOD. You are exalted as the Sovereign One.

I declare Jehovah Nissi over this land, for You are the one that causes victory over our enemies.

I declare Jehovah Saboath over this land, for You are the Lord of Hosts of angelic armies.

I declare the name Jehovah Rapha over this land for You are the One that heals.

I declare Jehovah Jireh over this land, for You are the one that provides.

I declare the name of El Gmulot, for You are the God of recompense and the one who spoils the plans of the enemy.

I declare the name of Jehovah Mekeddishkem over this land, for You are our sanctifier.

I declare the name of Jehovah Elohim over this land, for He is strong and causes men to fear the Lord.

I declare the name of Jehovah Adon over this land, for You are Master, Owner, Lord and covenant keeping God.

I declare the name of Jehovah Roi over this land, for the Lord is our Shepherd, protector and keeper.

I declare the name of Jehovah Shammah, for the Lord is present.

I declare the name of Jehovah Tdiskenu over this land for You are our righteousness.

I declare the name of Jehovah Shalom over this land, for You are our peace. I release the Spirit of Adoption over every individual and household, to draw people into personal relationship with the Lord Jesus Christ and to shed abroad the revelation of Abba Father in the hearts of every individual, in Jesus name.

I ask now, Father, for angelic assistance to be released to open the heavens and release breakthrough in this land, in this city and throughout this nation. I thank you for hearing my prayer and declarations, and establishing them for us so that light will shine on our ways. This you have promised in Job 22:28, and I thank You for watching over Your word to perform it.

Lord Jesus, you also promised in Your word that where two or more are praying in agreement then You are in our midst and whatever we have asked, You will do. I know that others are in agreement with this prayer; join our prayers together. As we have declared these things then we expect You to release angelic assistance to enforce our prayers and declarations. I expect you to enforce the submission and eviction of the enemy, and I thank You for it, in Jesus name. Amen.

ABOUT THE AUTHOR

Laura Gagnon is a woman who understands the power of God to heal and deliver. Once bound by emotional pain, bitterness and oppressed by the enemy, she now works with others helping them to receive healing and deliverance through Jesus Christ. She is the author of *Healing the Heart of a Woman, Prayers for Impossible Situations,* and co-author of her husband's book, *Room to Grow*. Laura also writes for her blog, **Beyond the Barriers**. Laura and her husband, Norm, are ministers of the gospel and live with their children in Escondido, California.

Made in the USA
Columbia, SC
06 March 2019